WONDERFUL

WILDLIFE

COLORING BOOK

Pen & Ink Artwork by Brenda Potts

www.BooksByPotts.com

Background Cover Illustration by novielysa

ThinkStockPhotos.com by Getty Images

ISBN 978-0-9883272-3-8

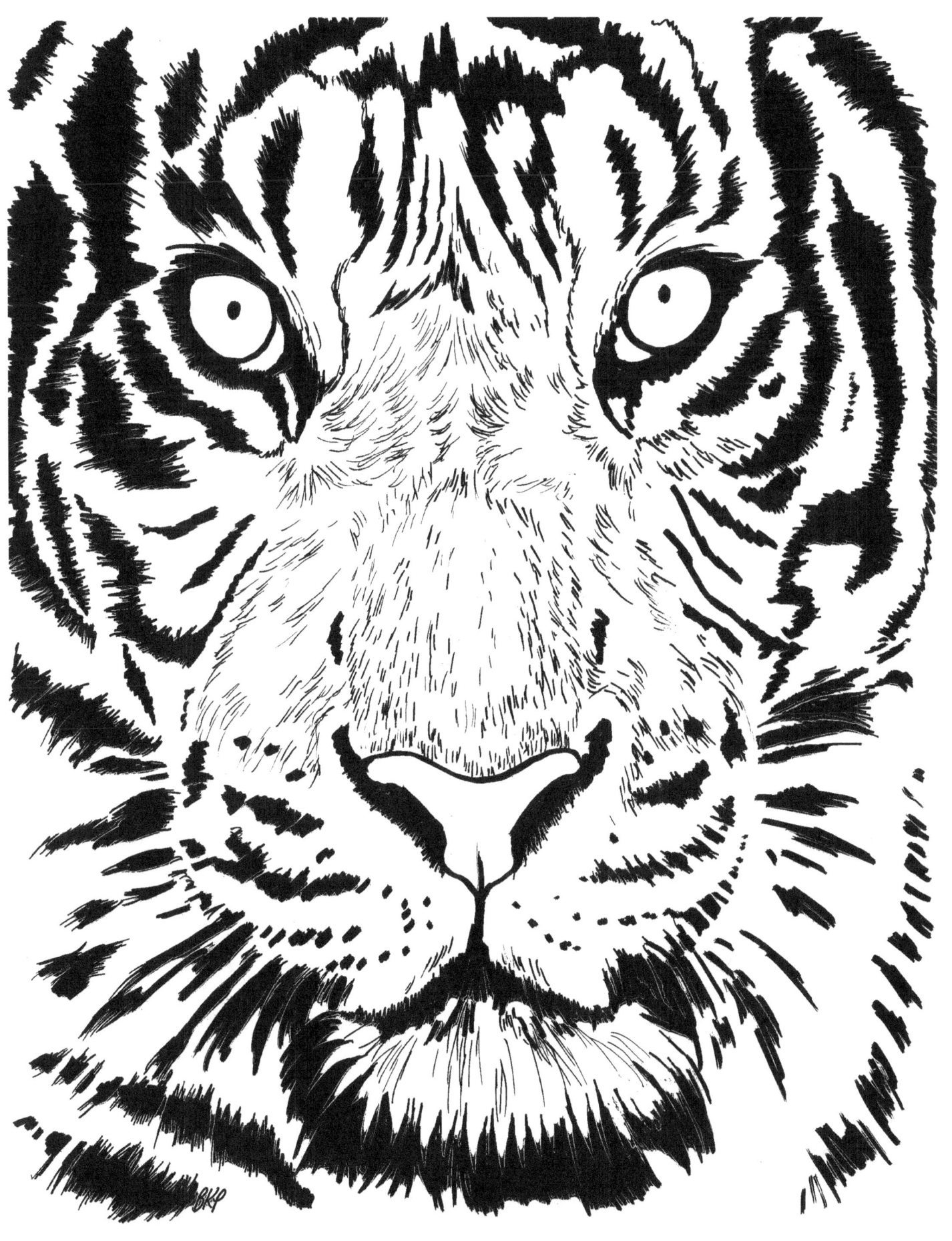

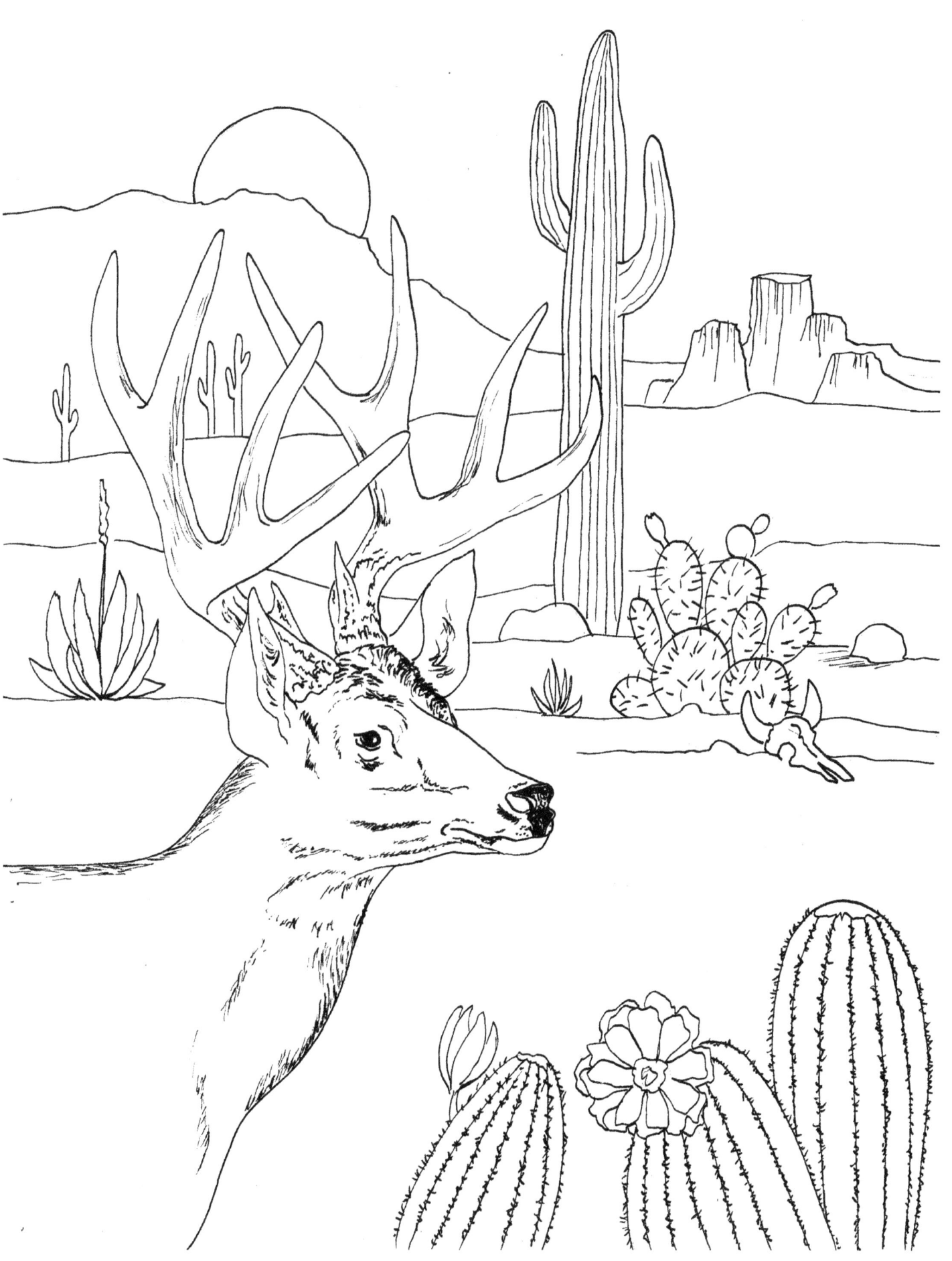

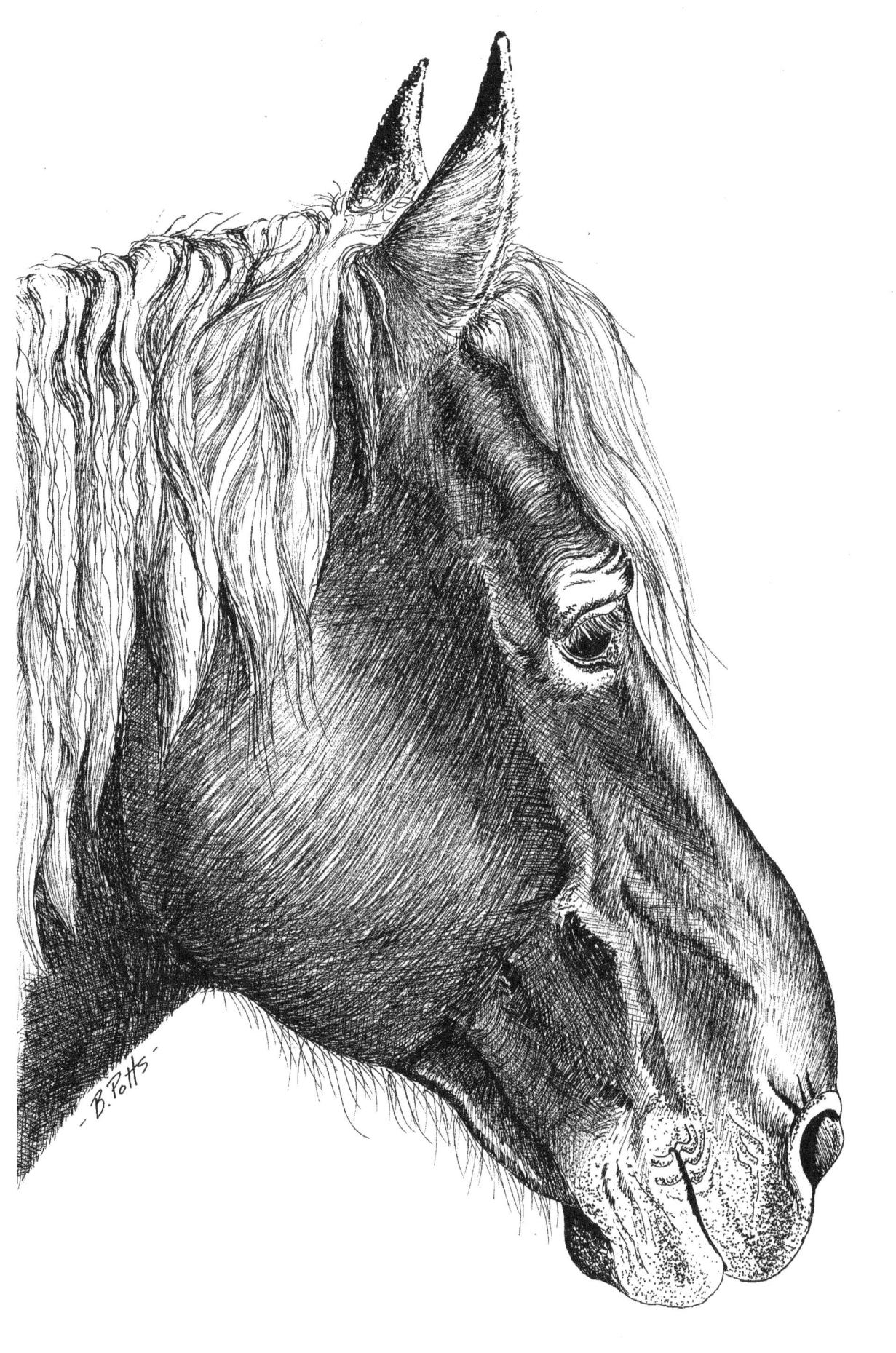

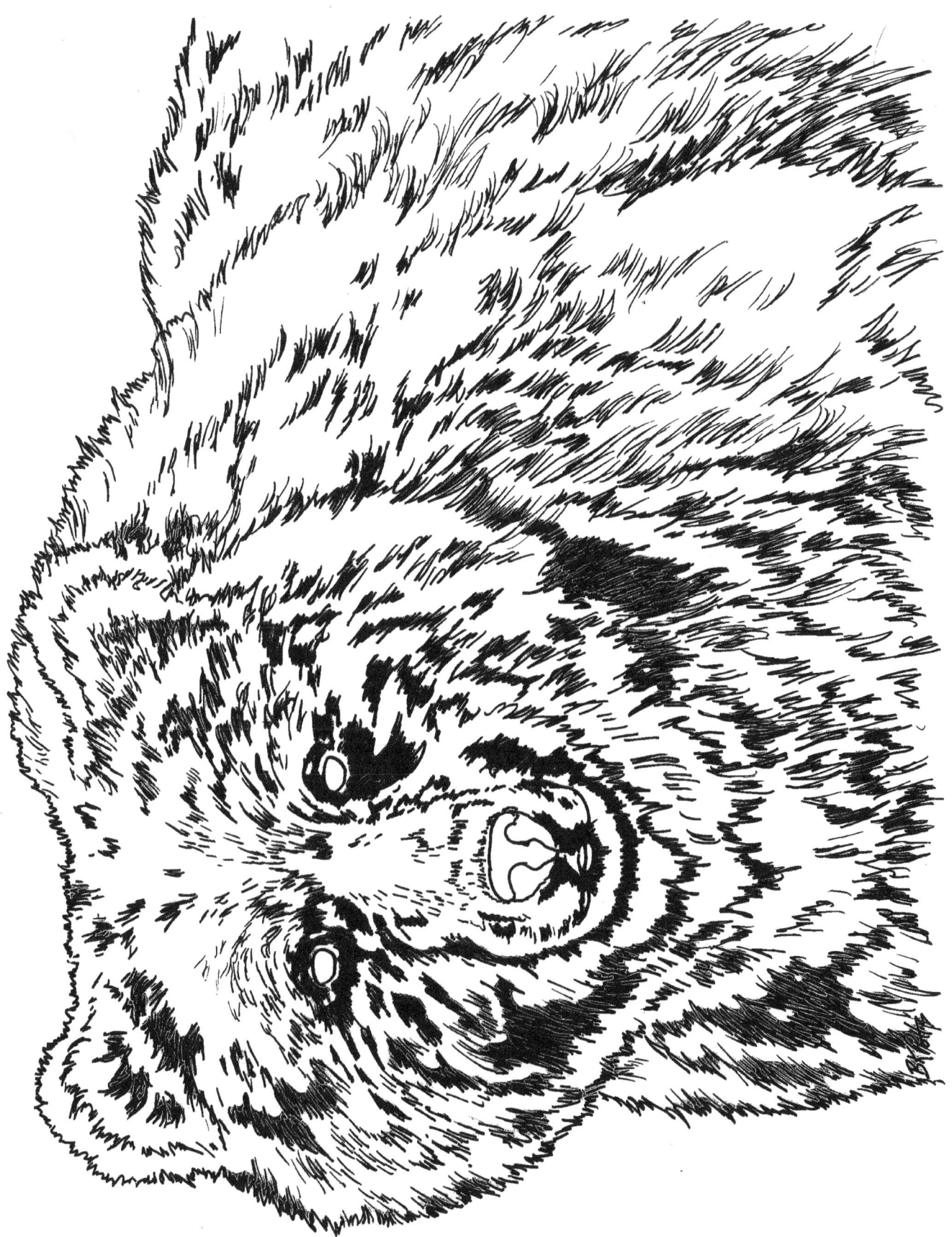

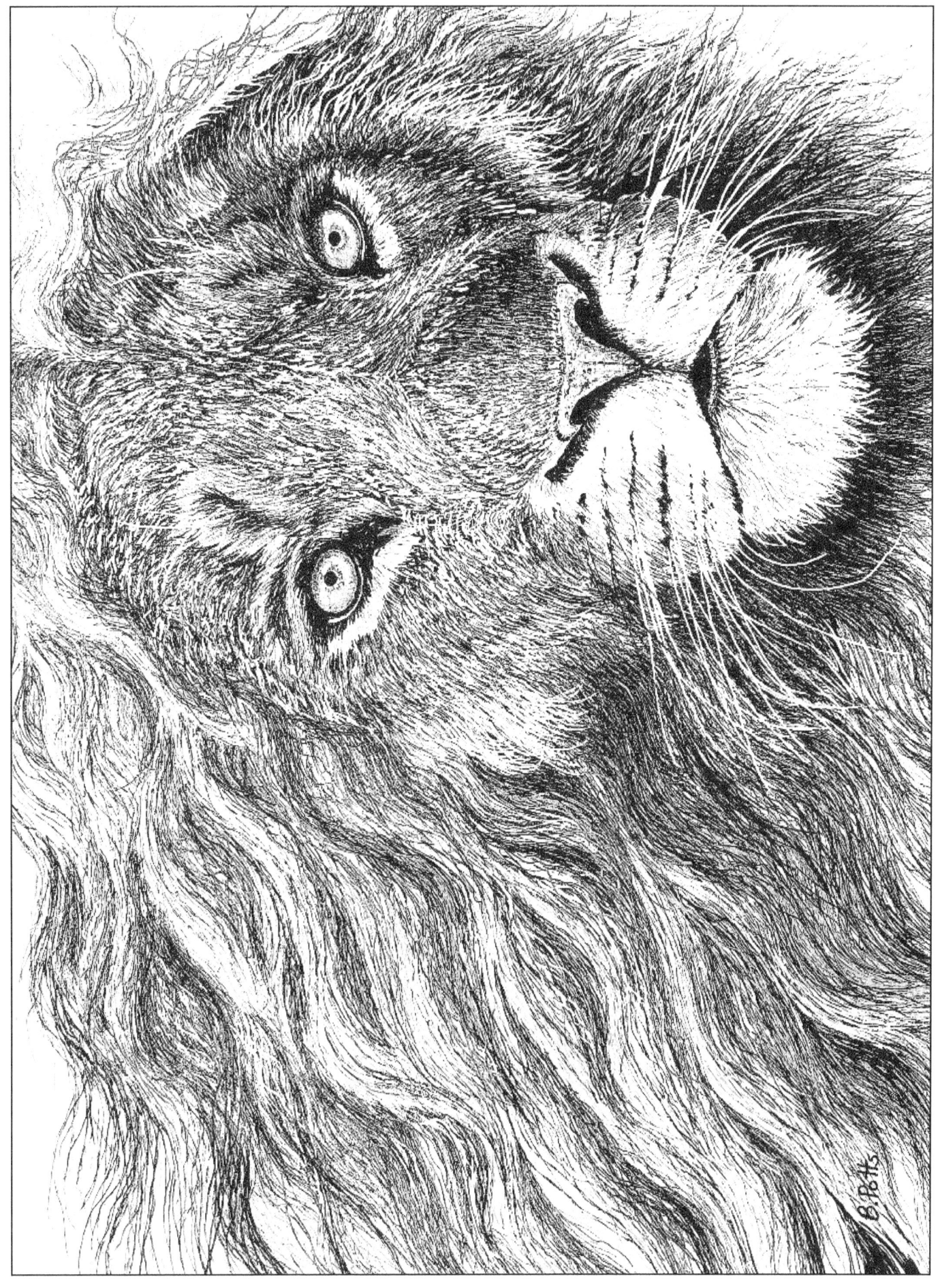

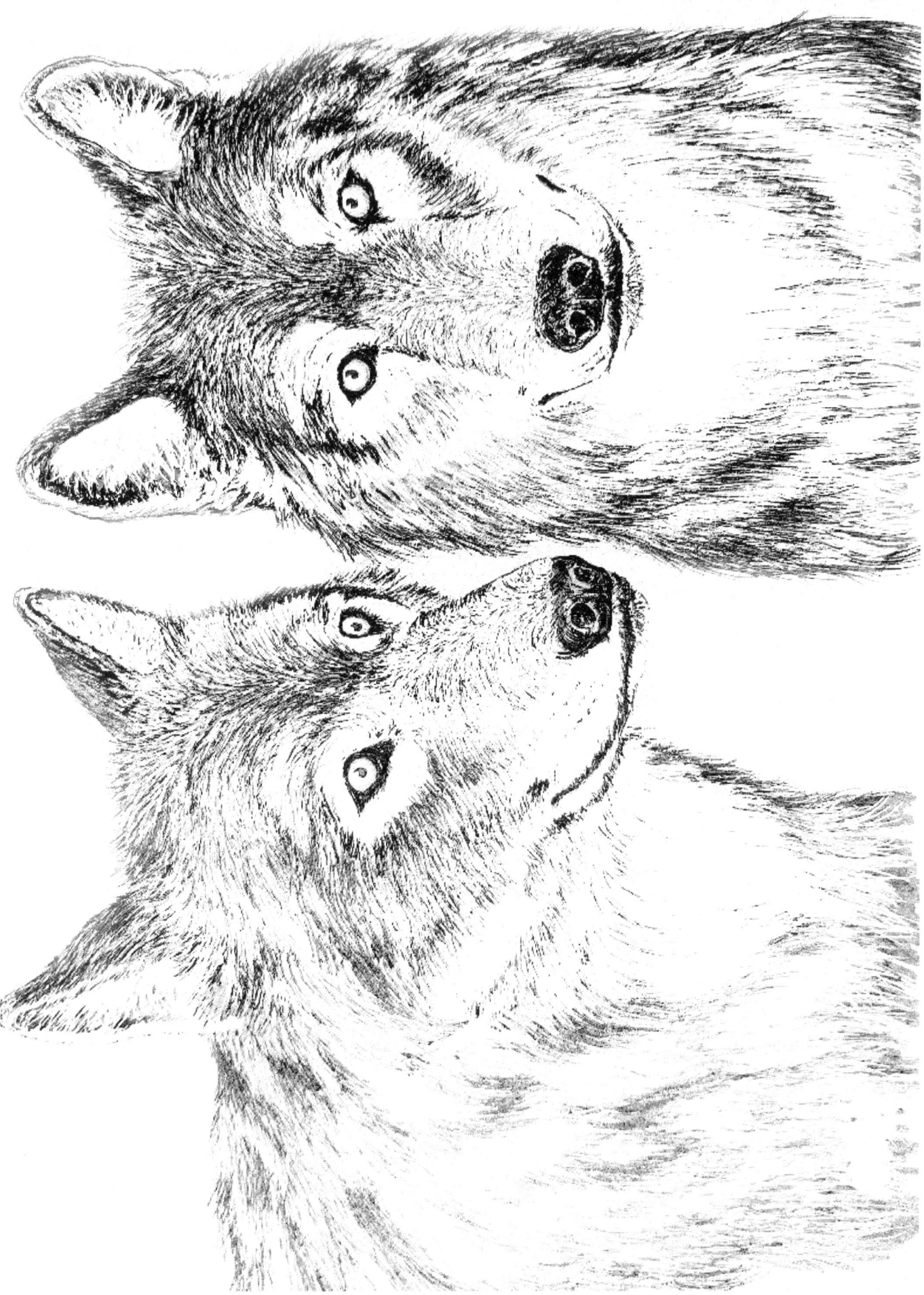

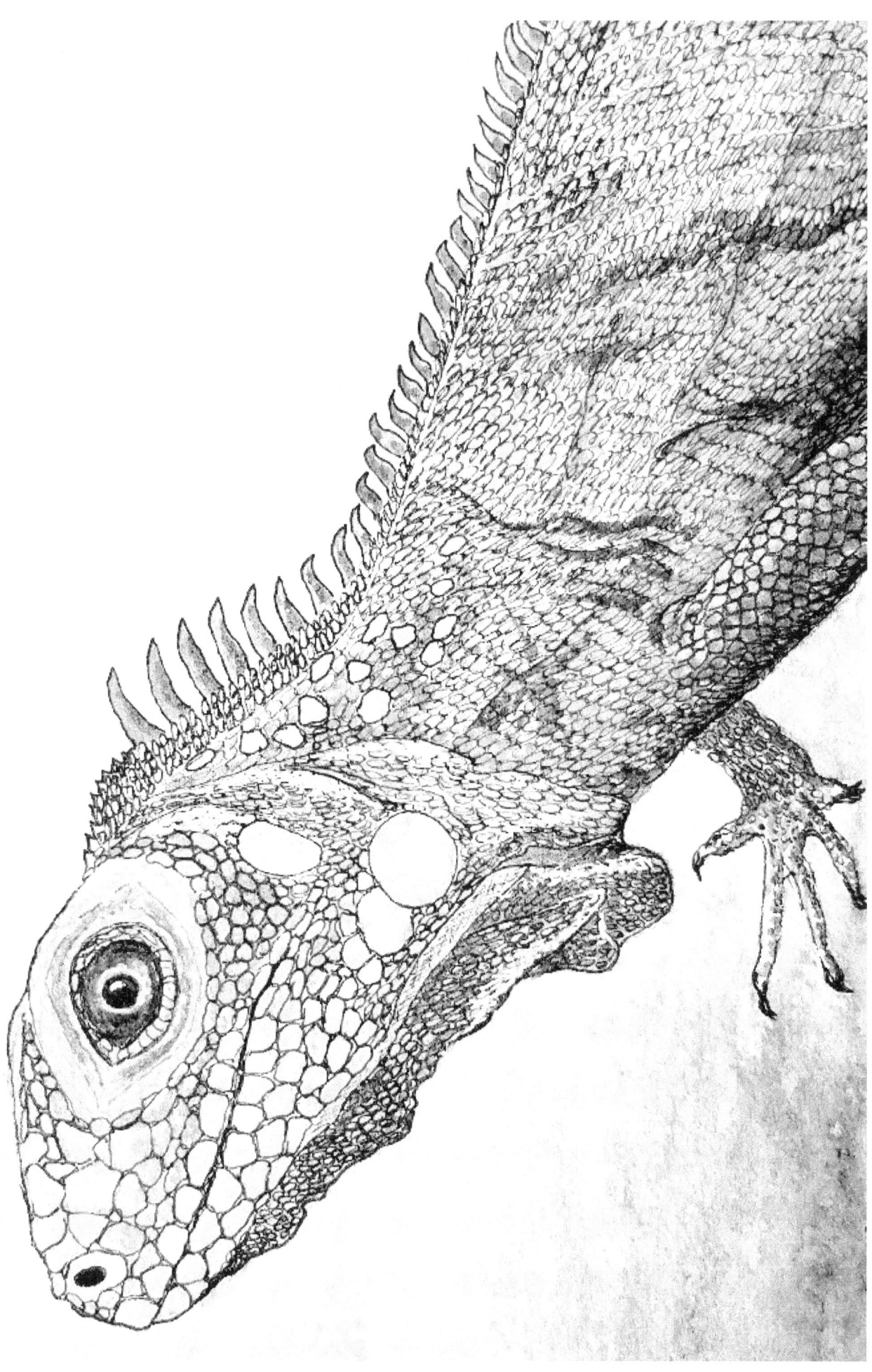

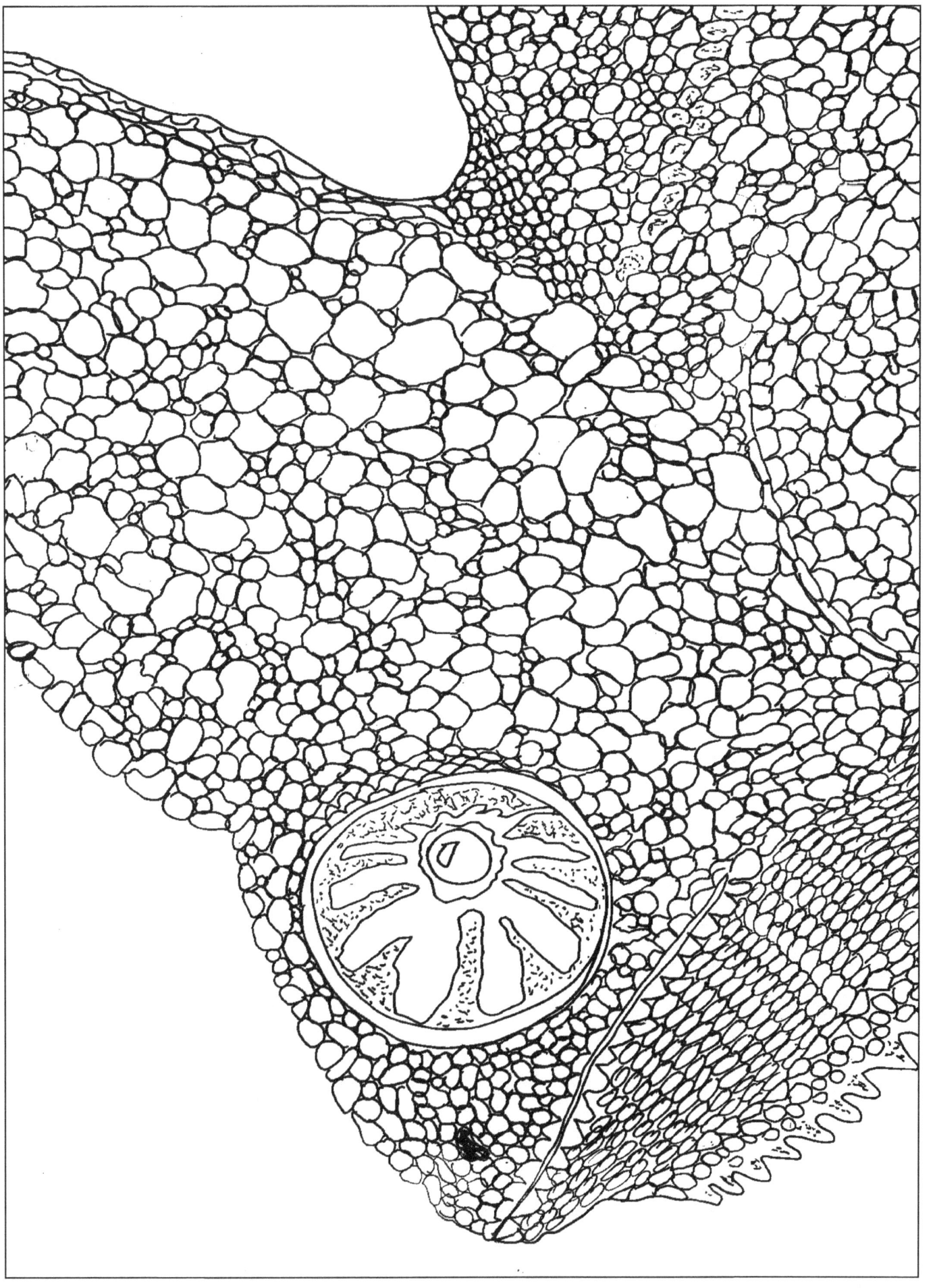

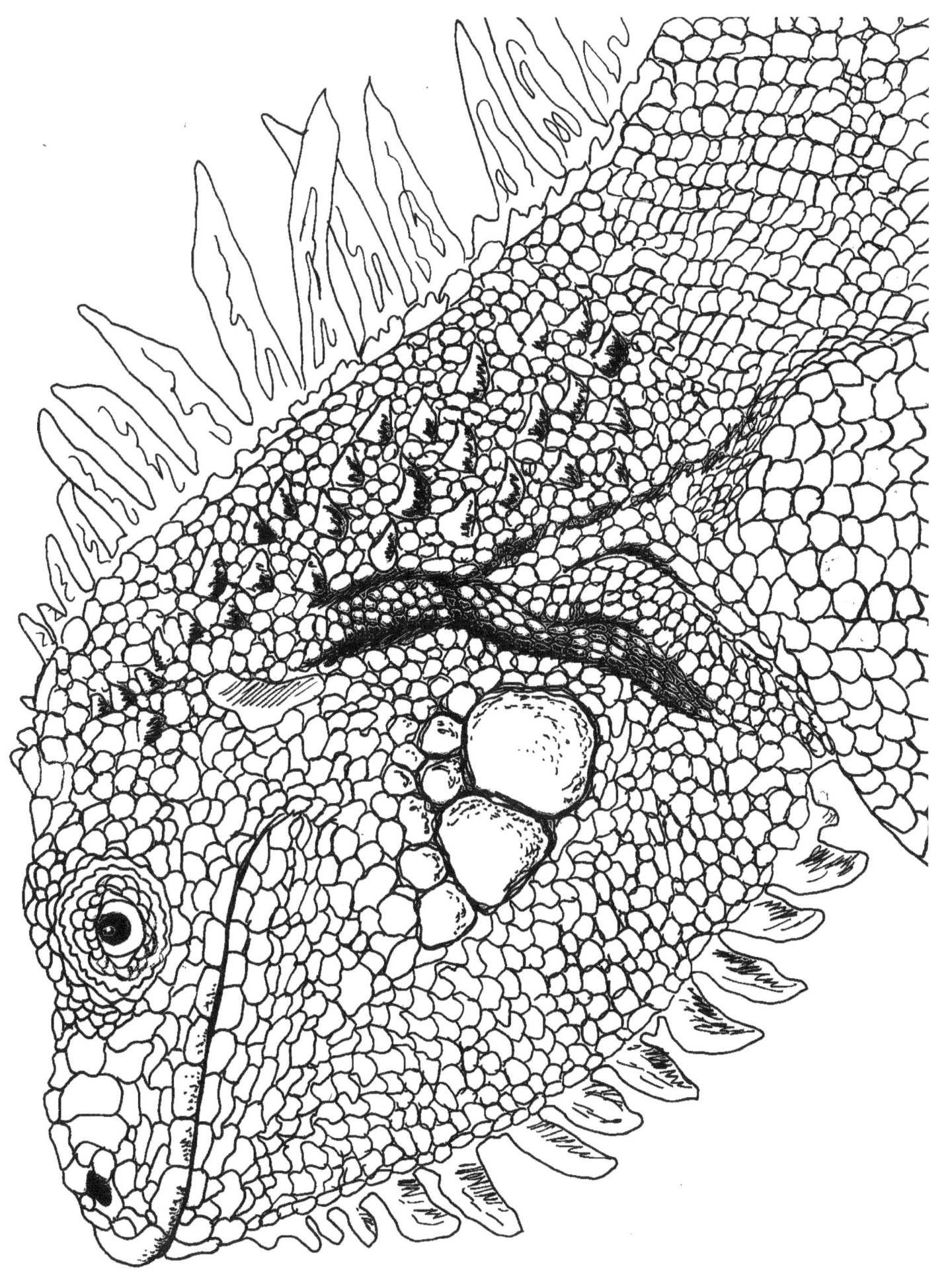

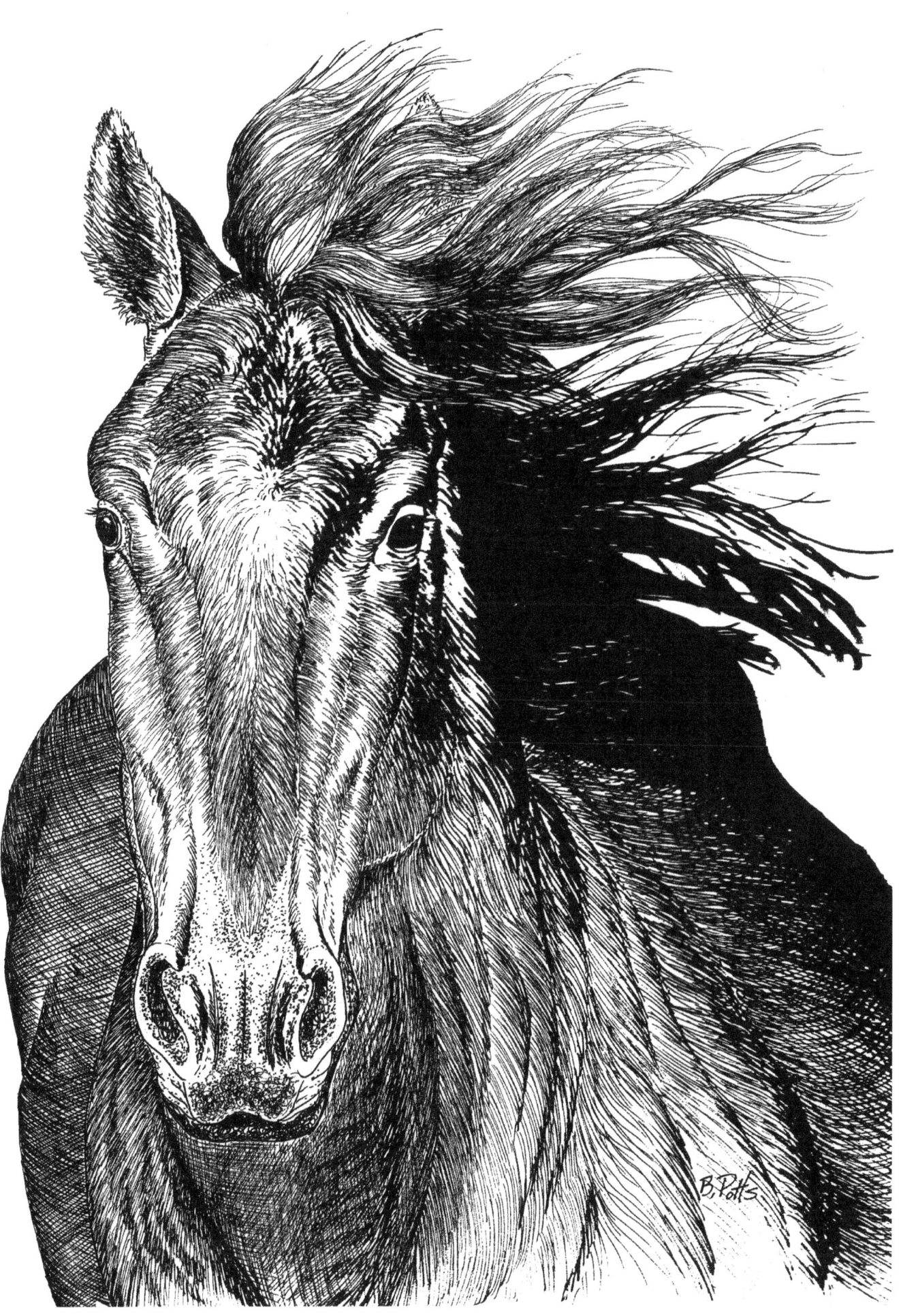

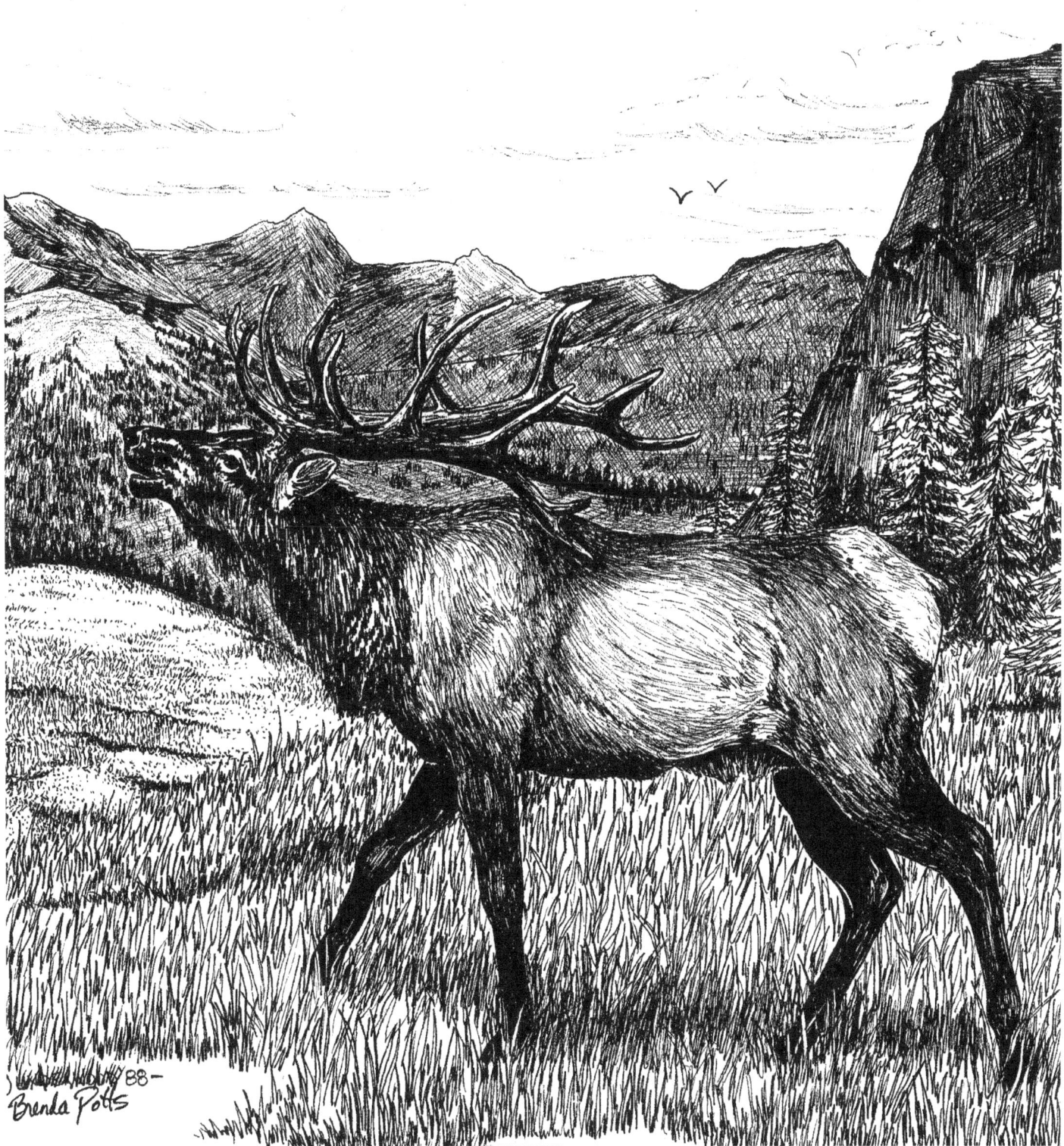

Brenda Potts

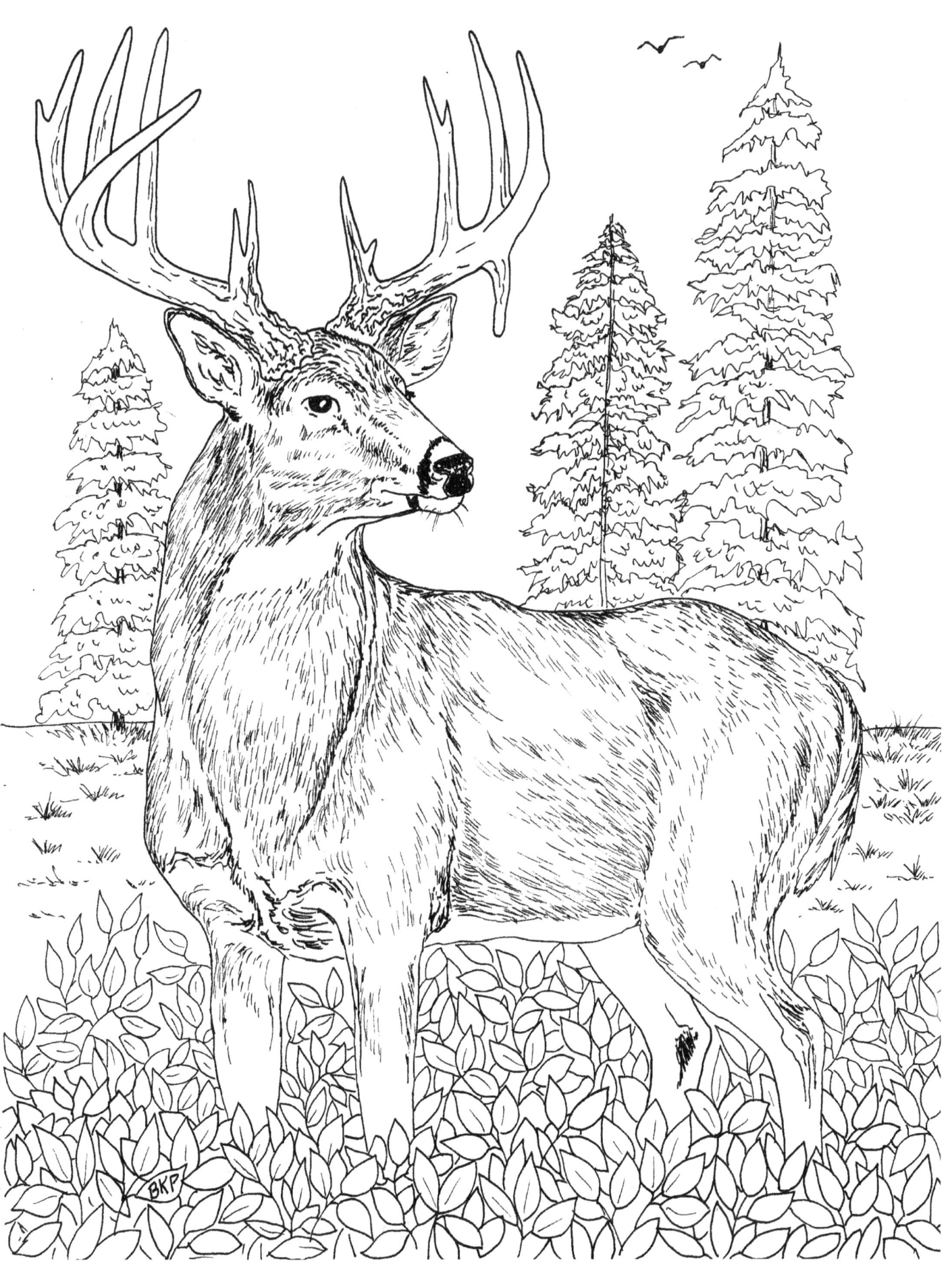

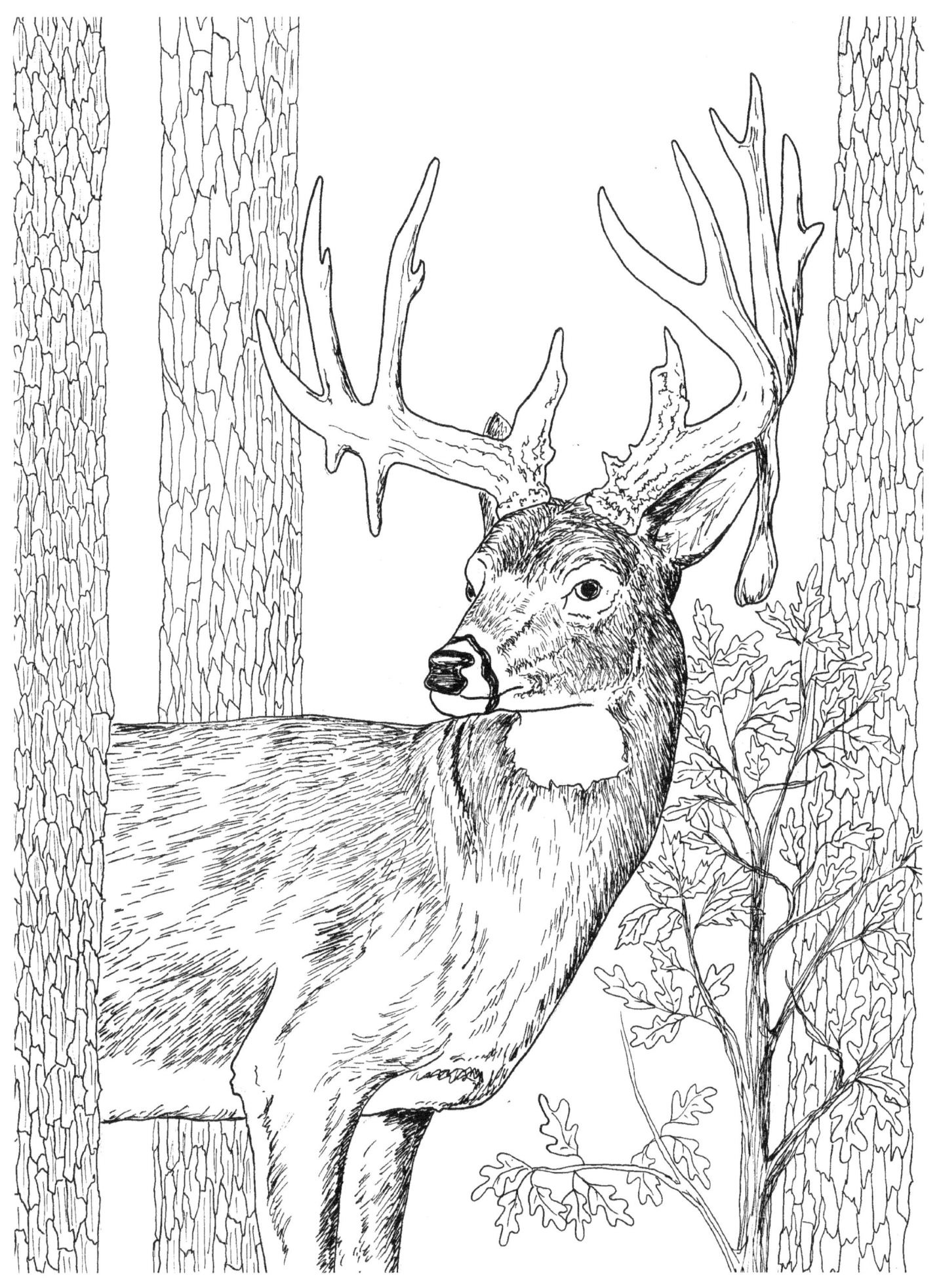

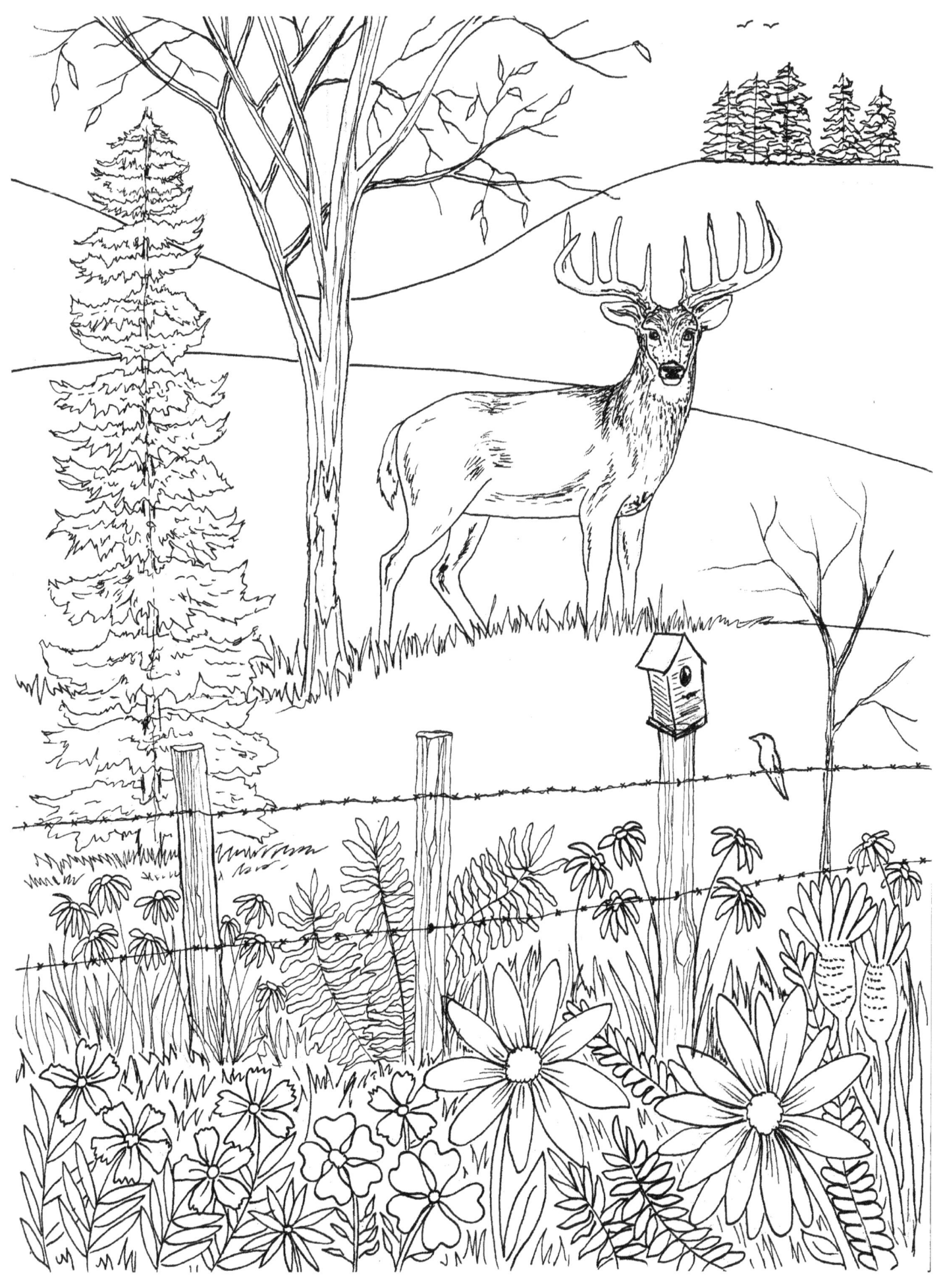

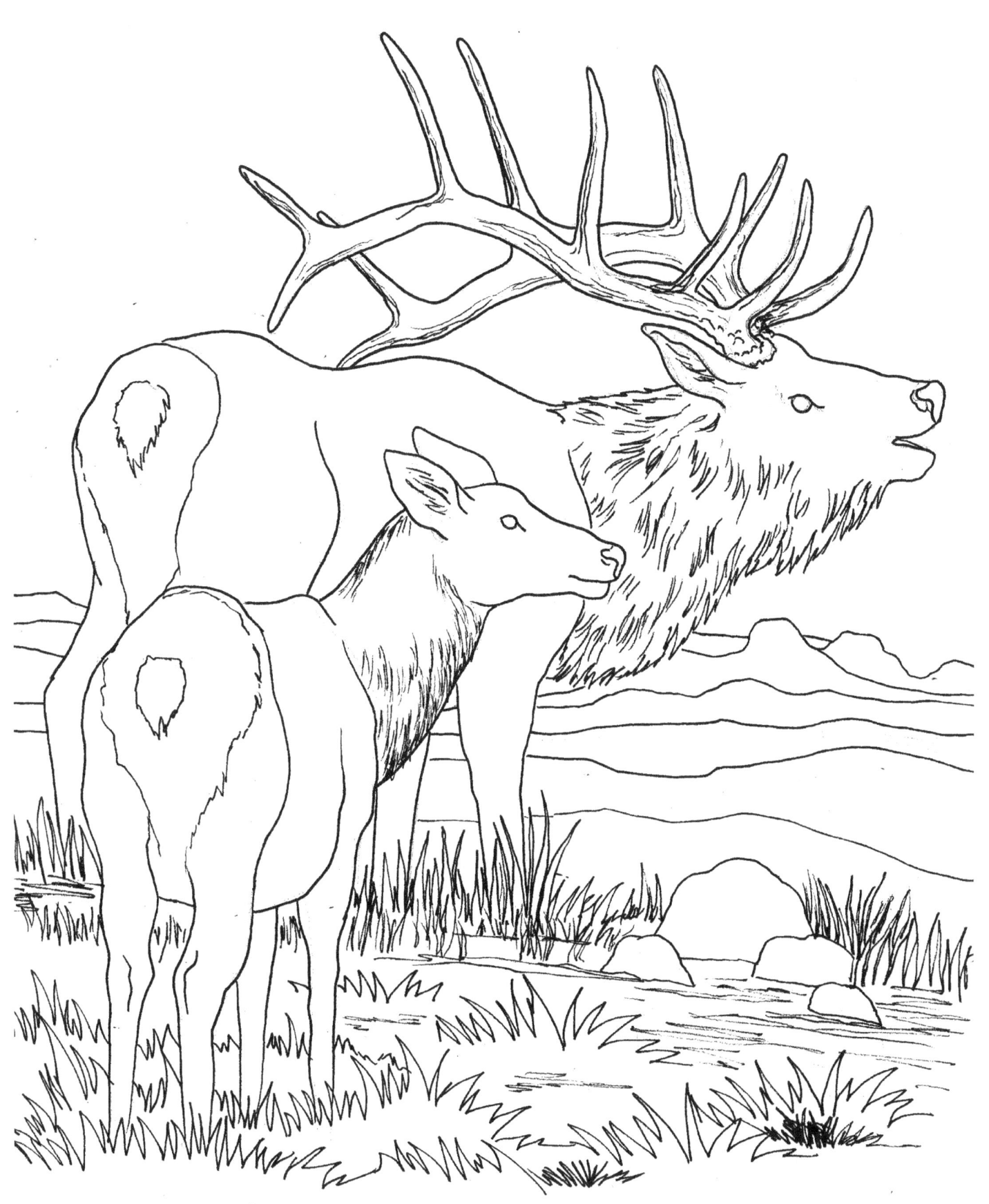

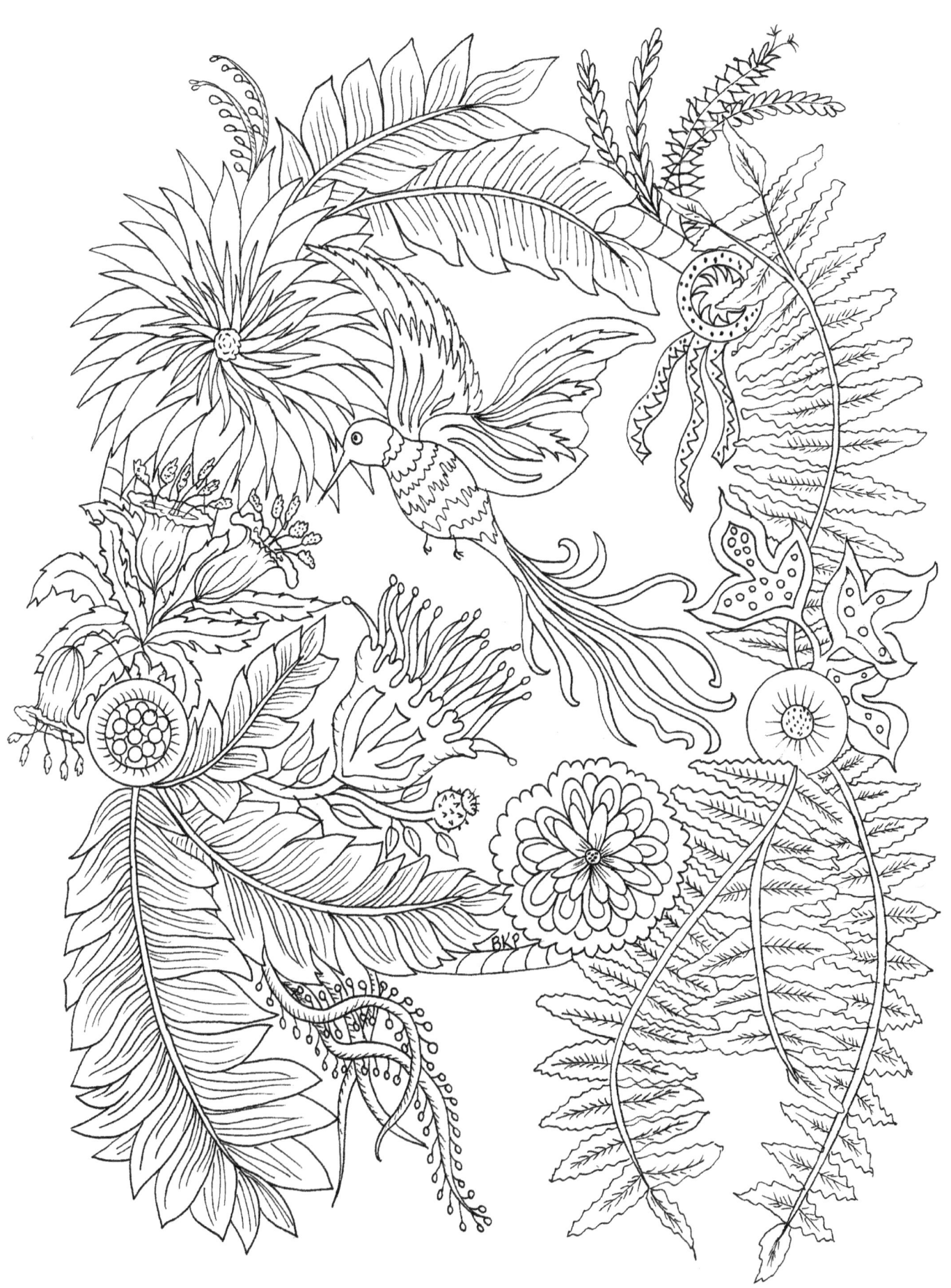

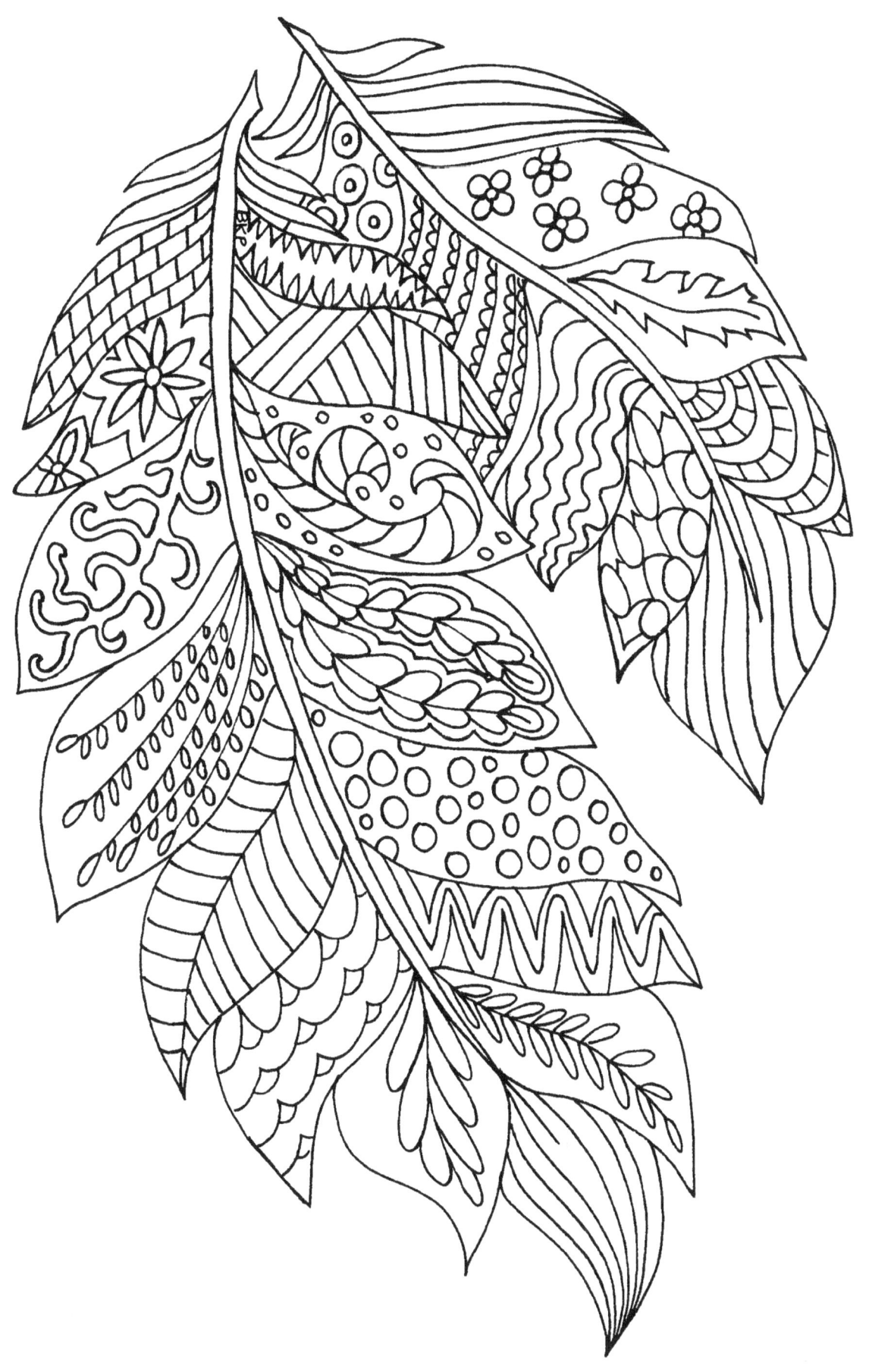

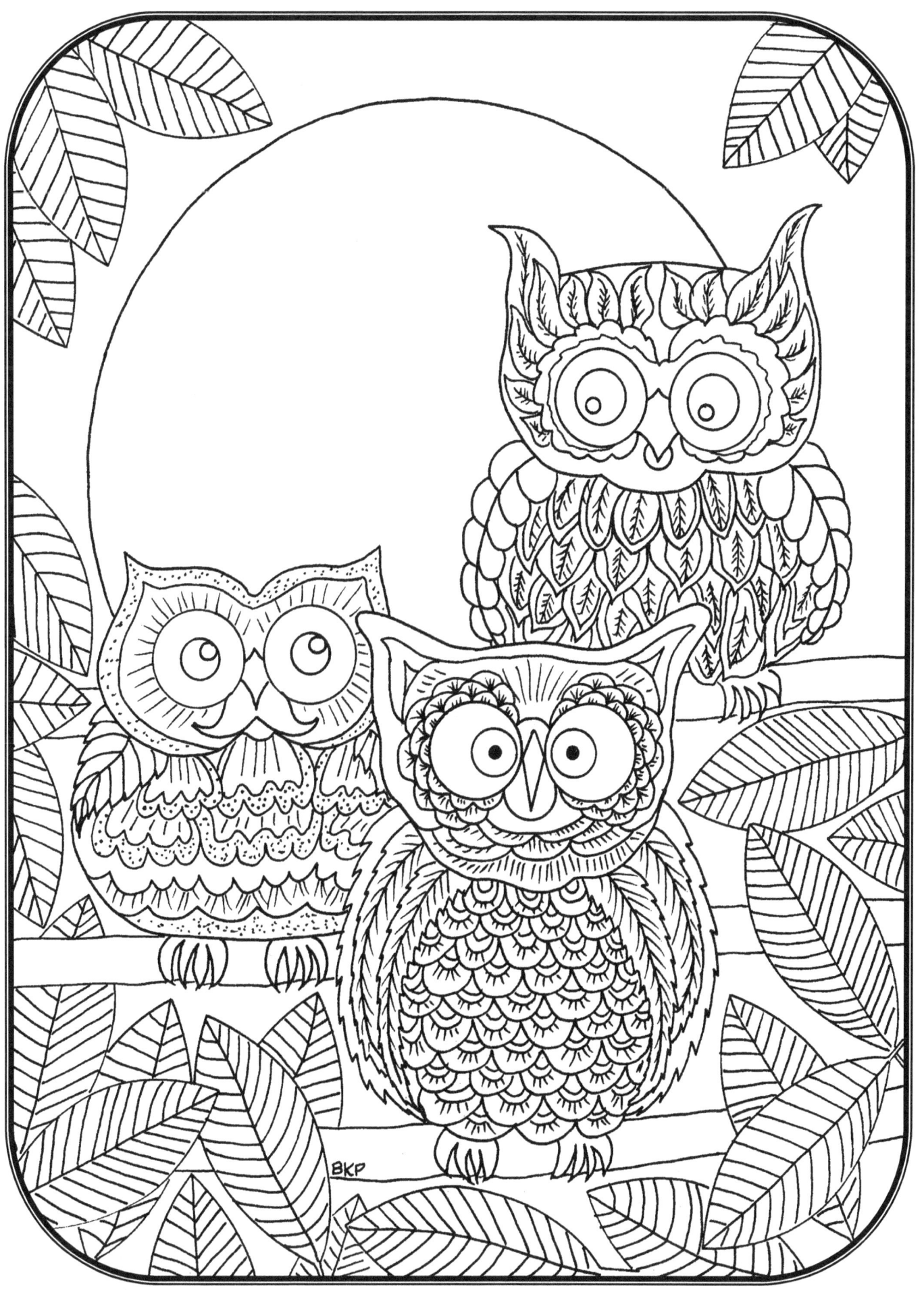

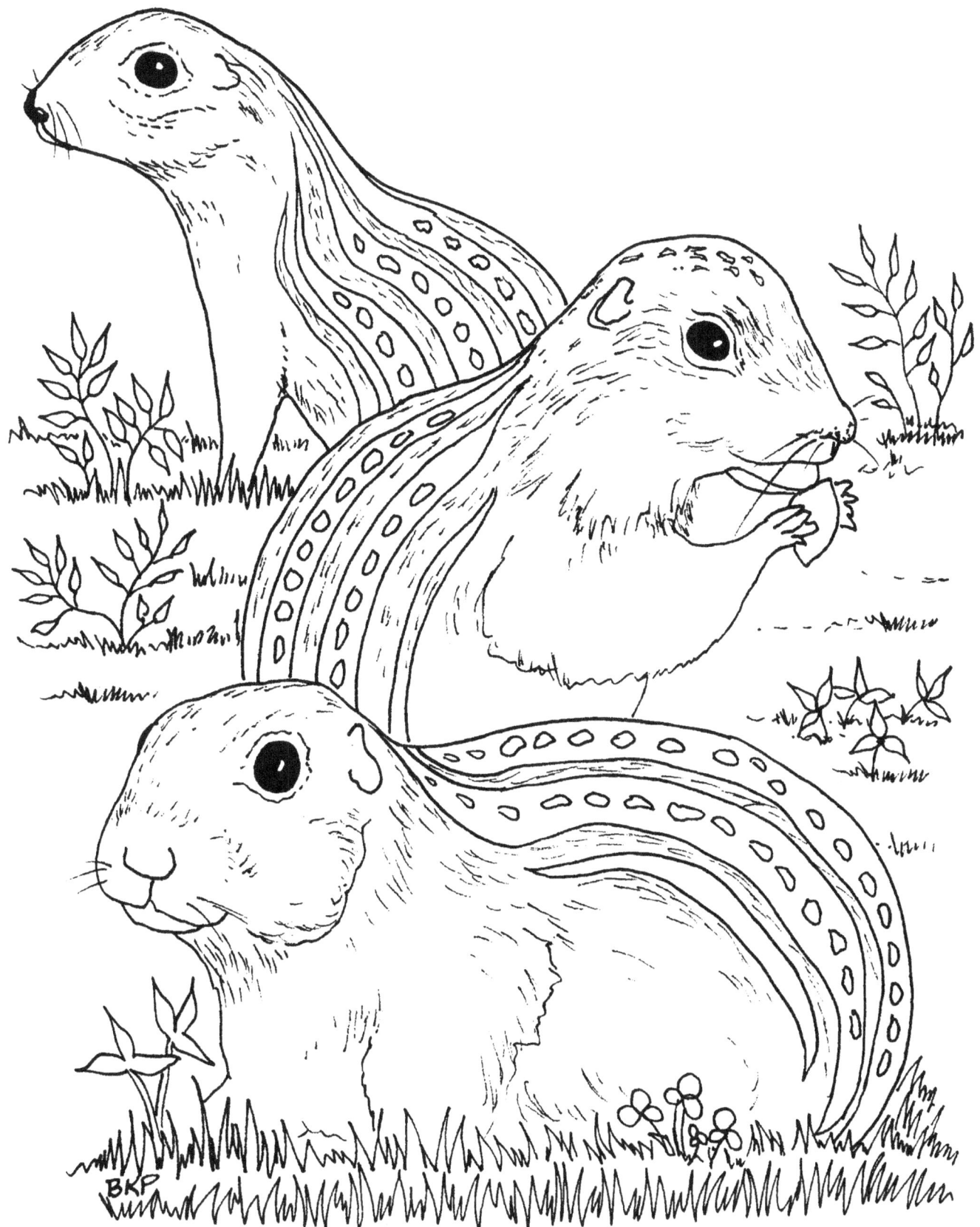

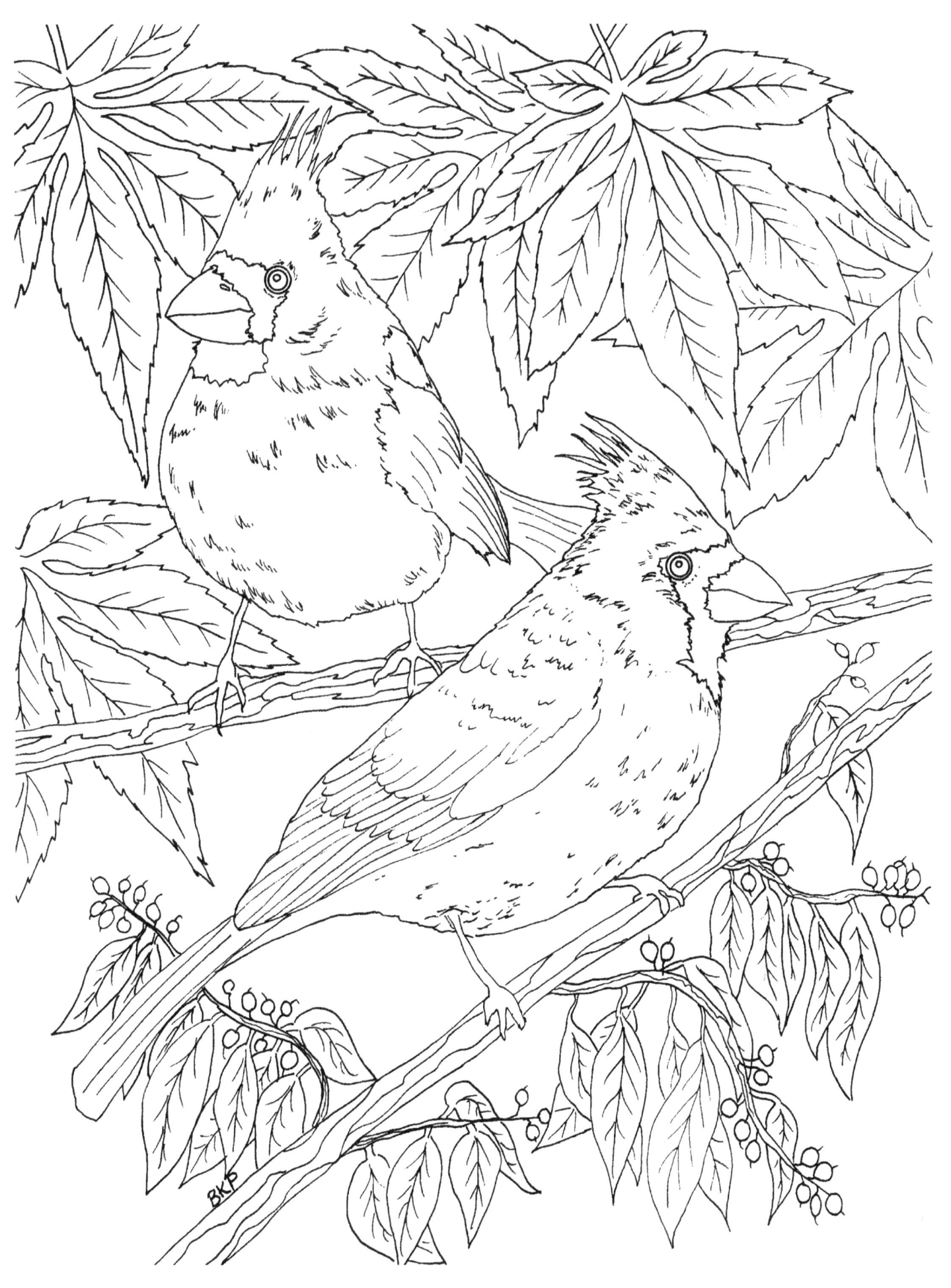

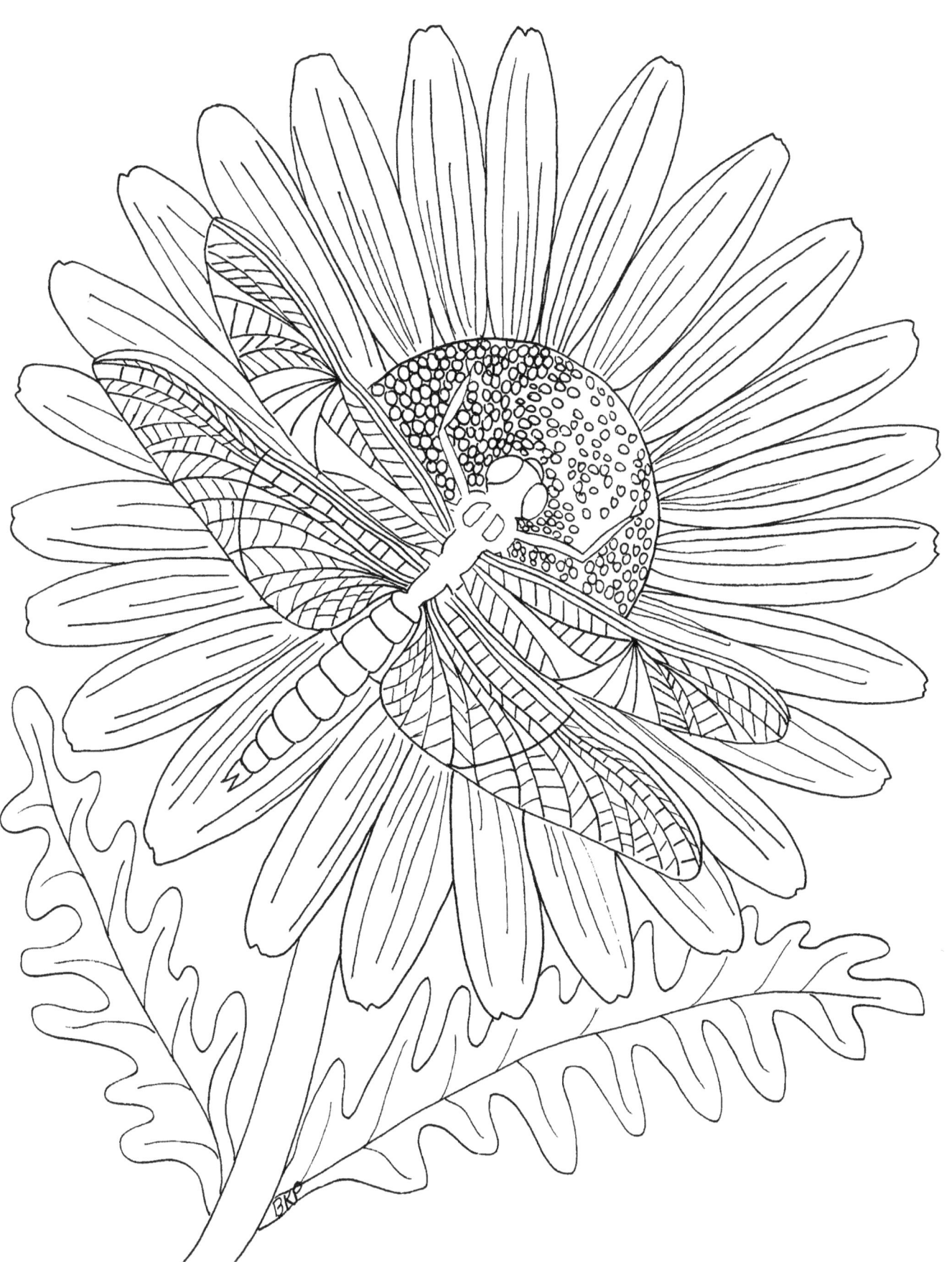

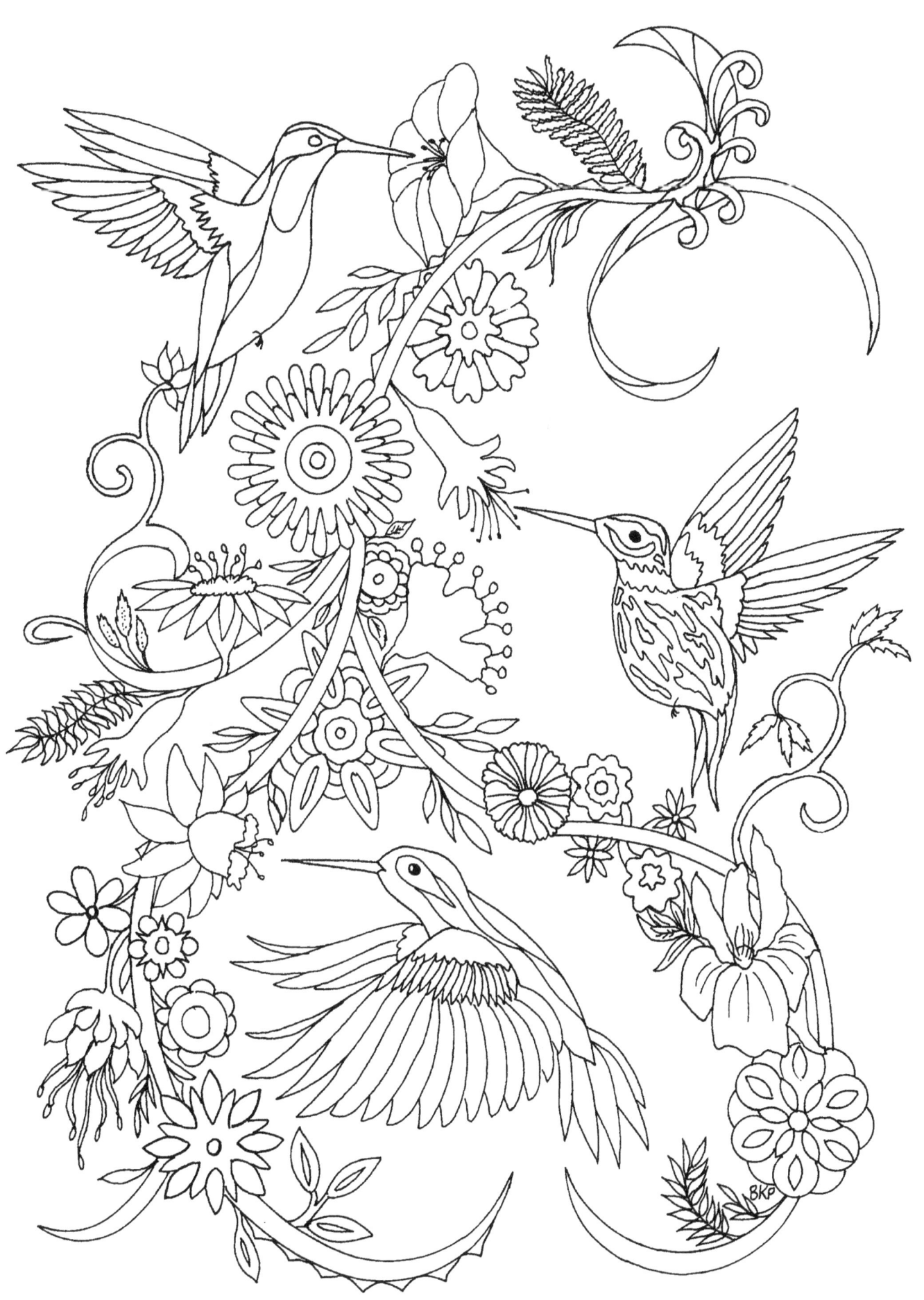

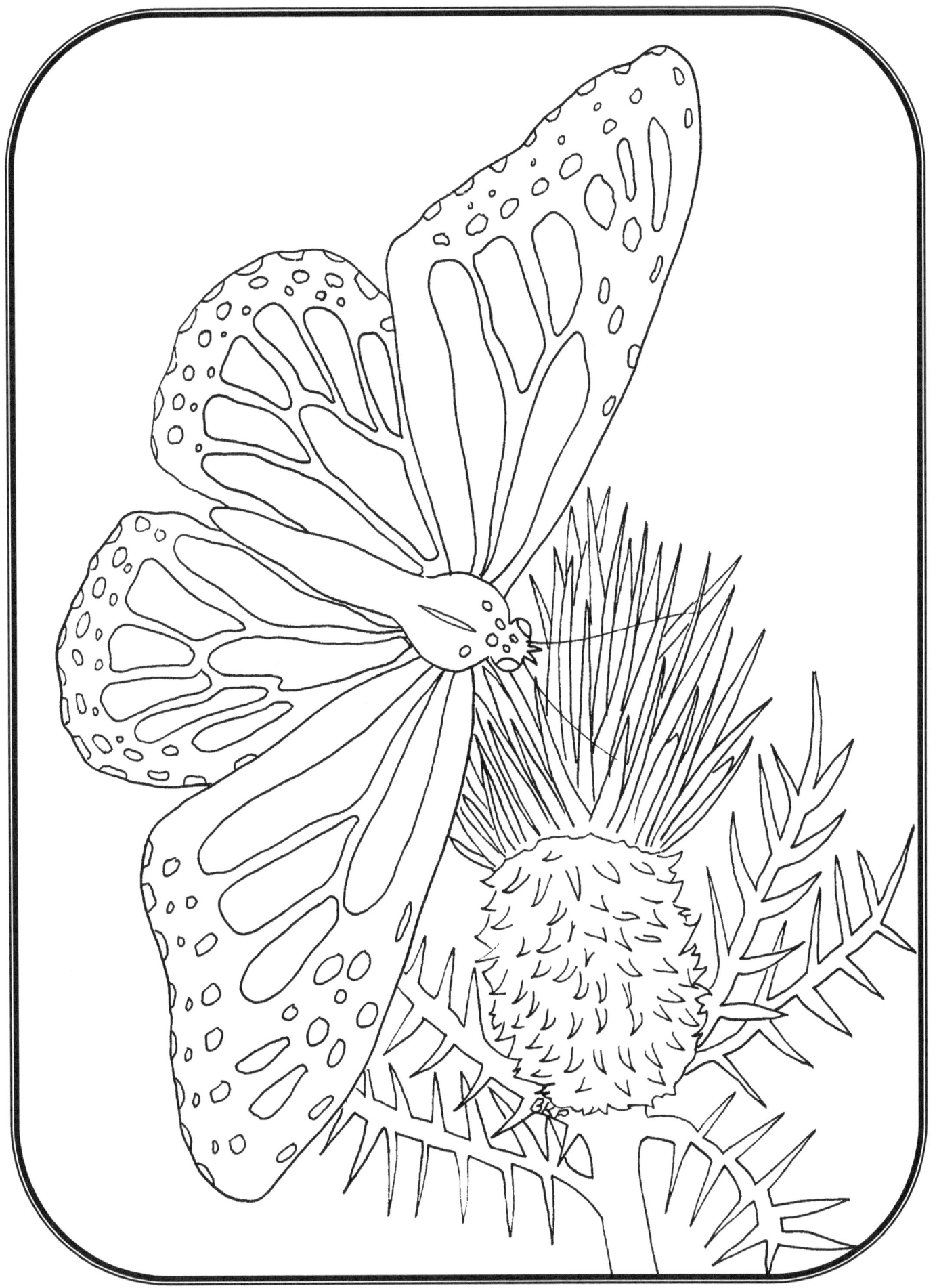

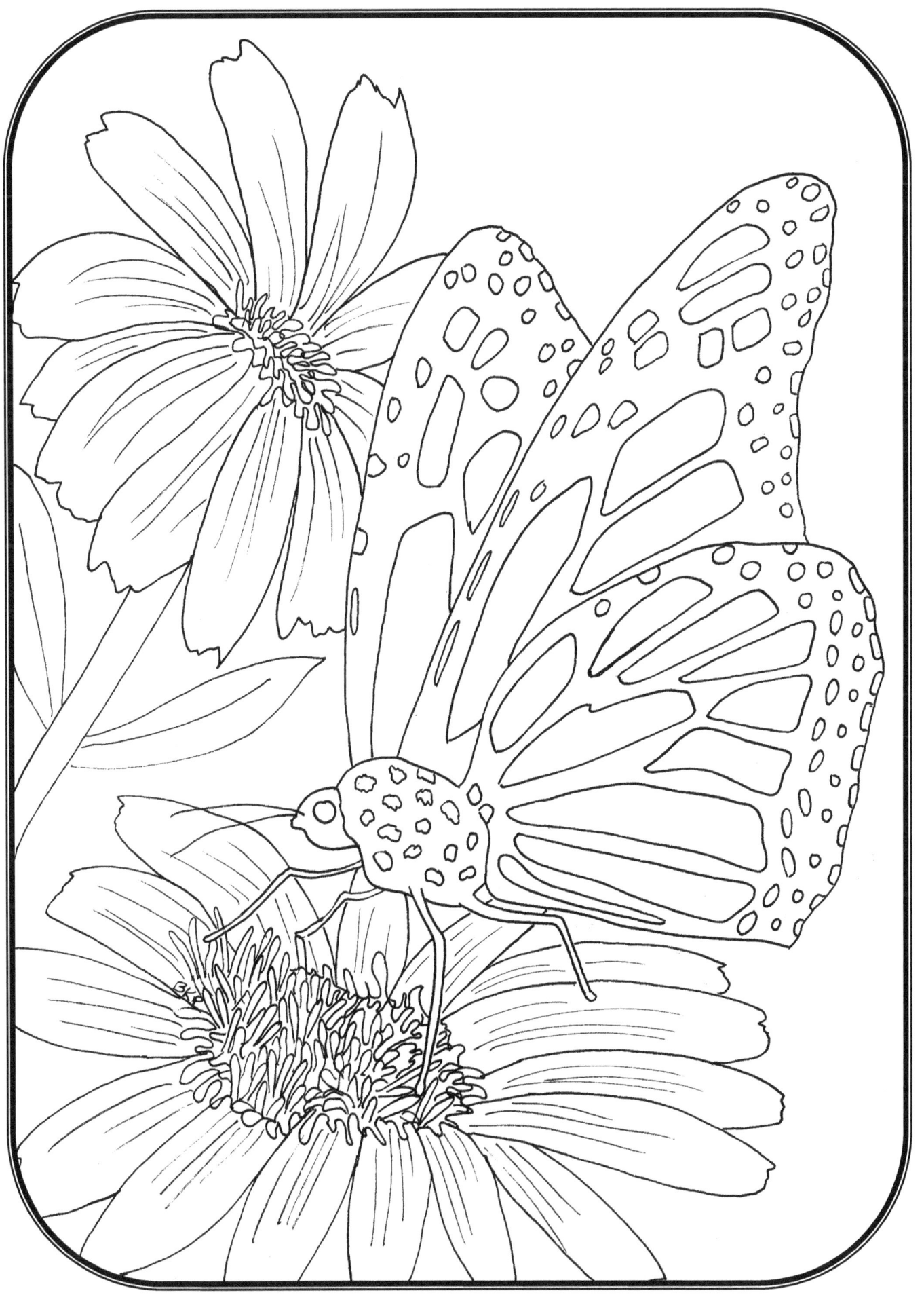

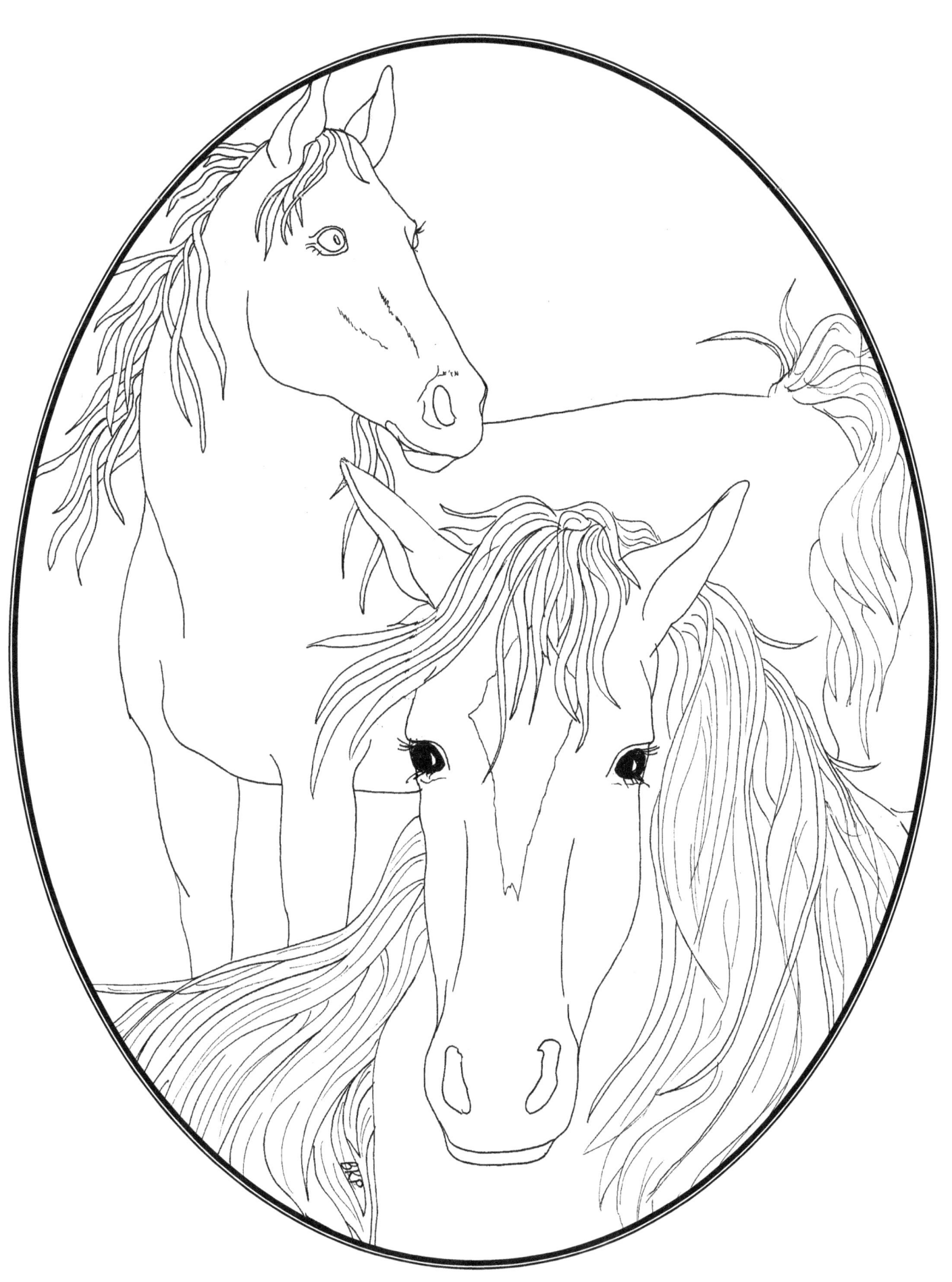

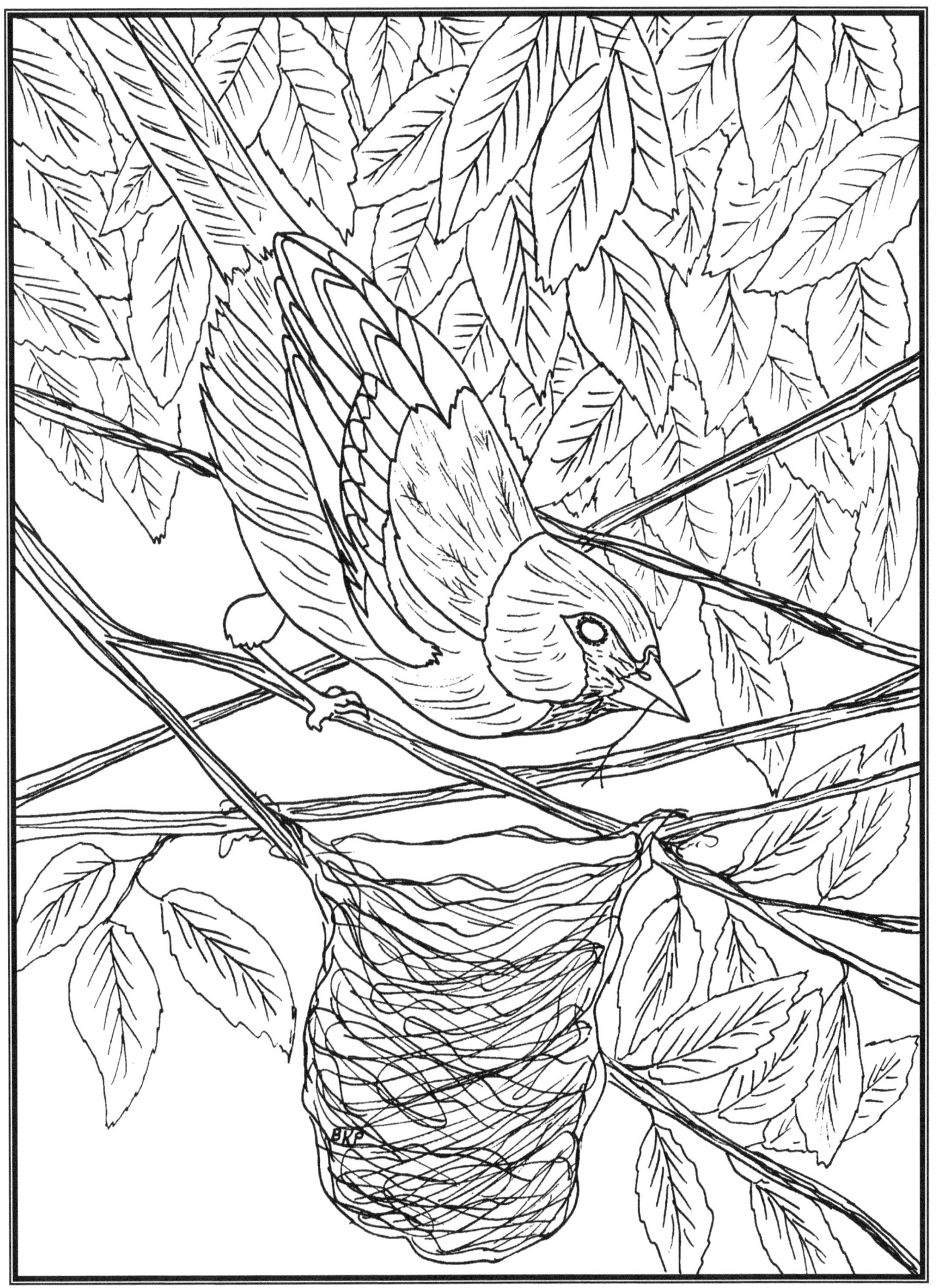

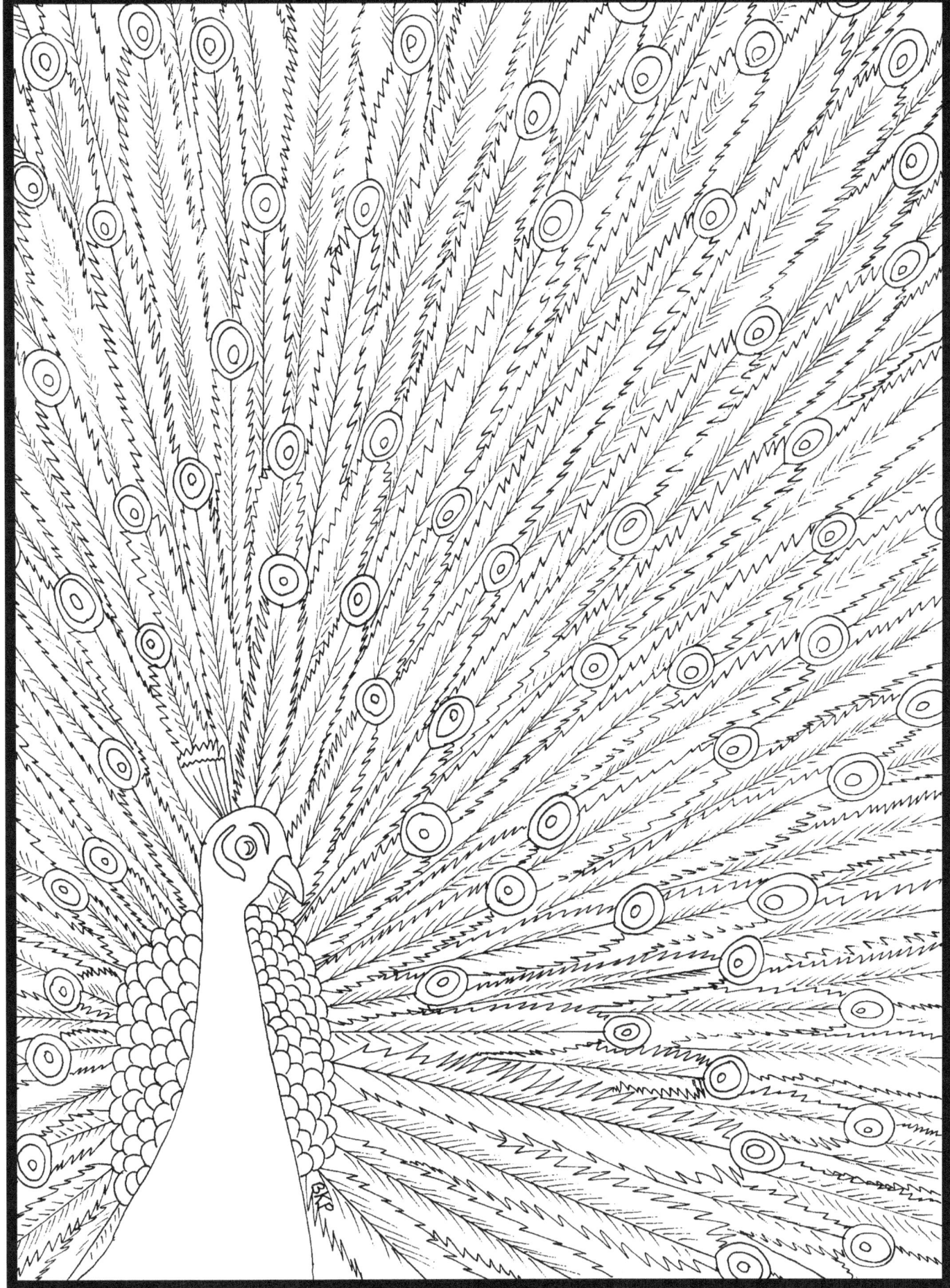

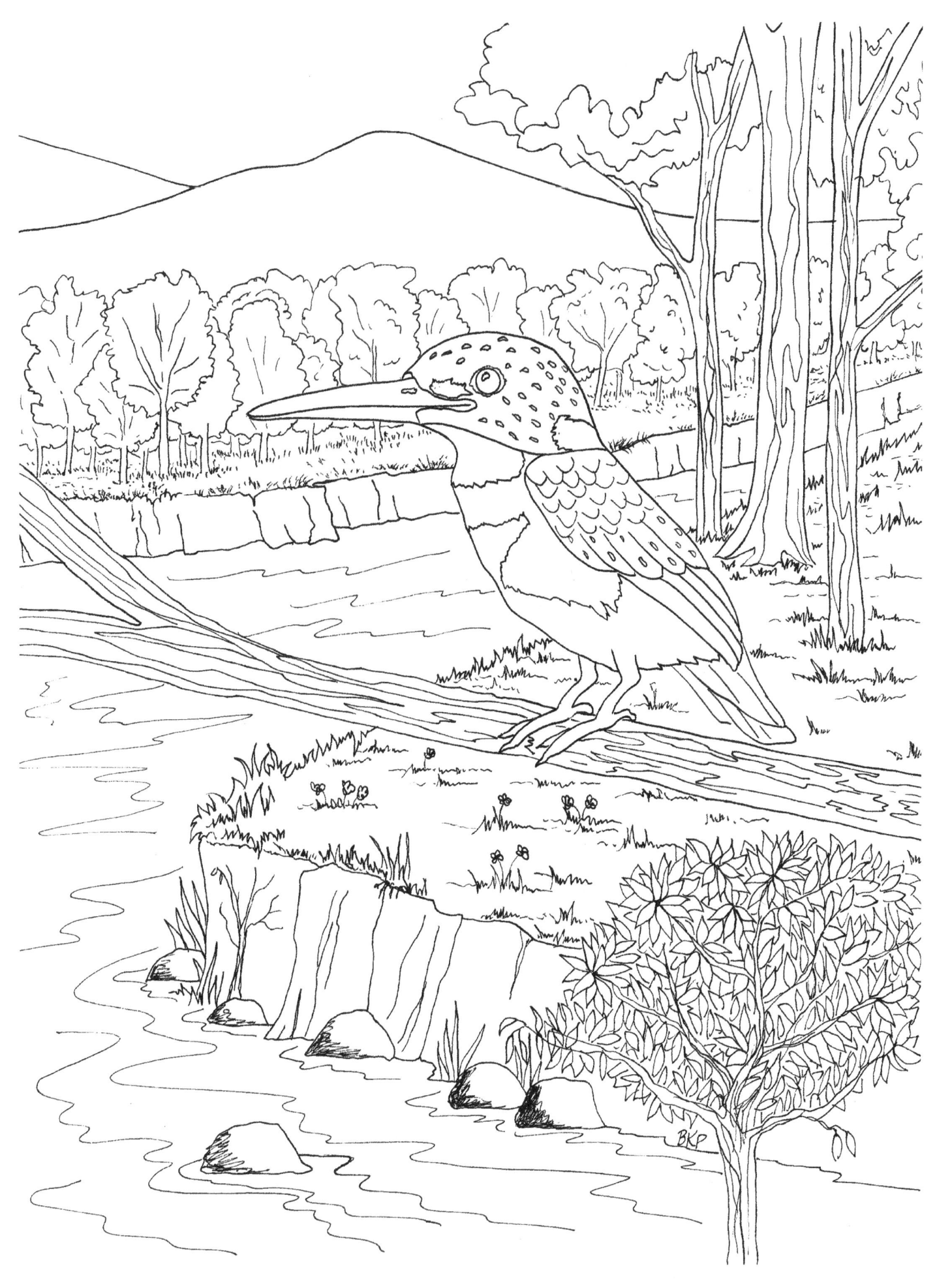

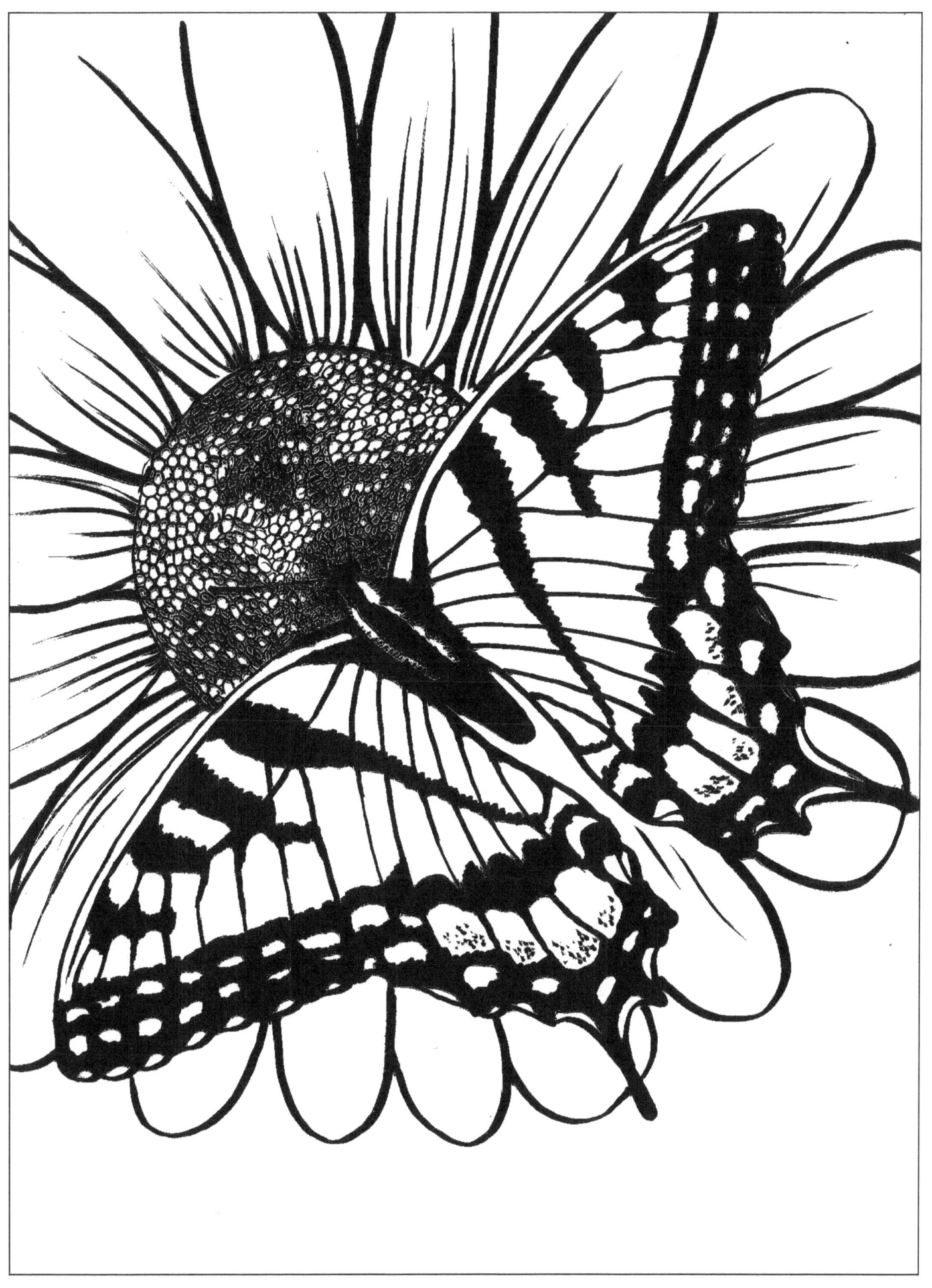

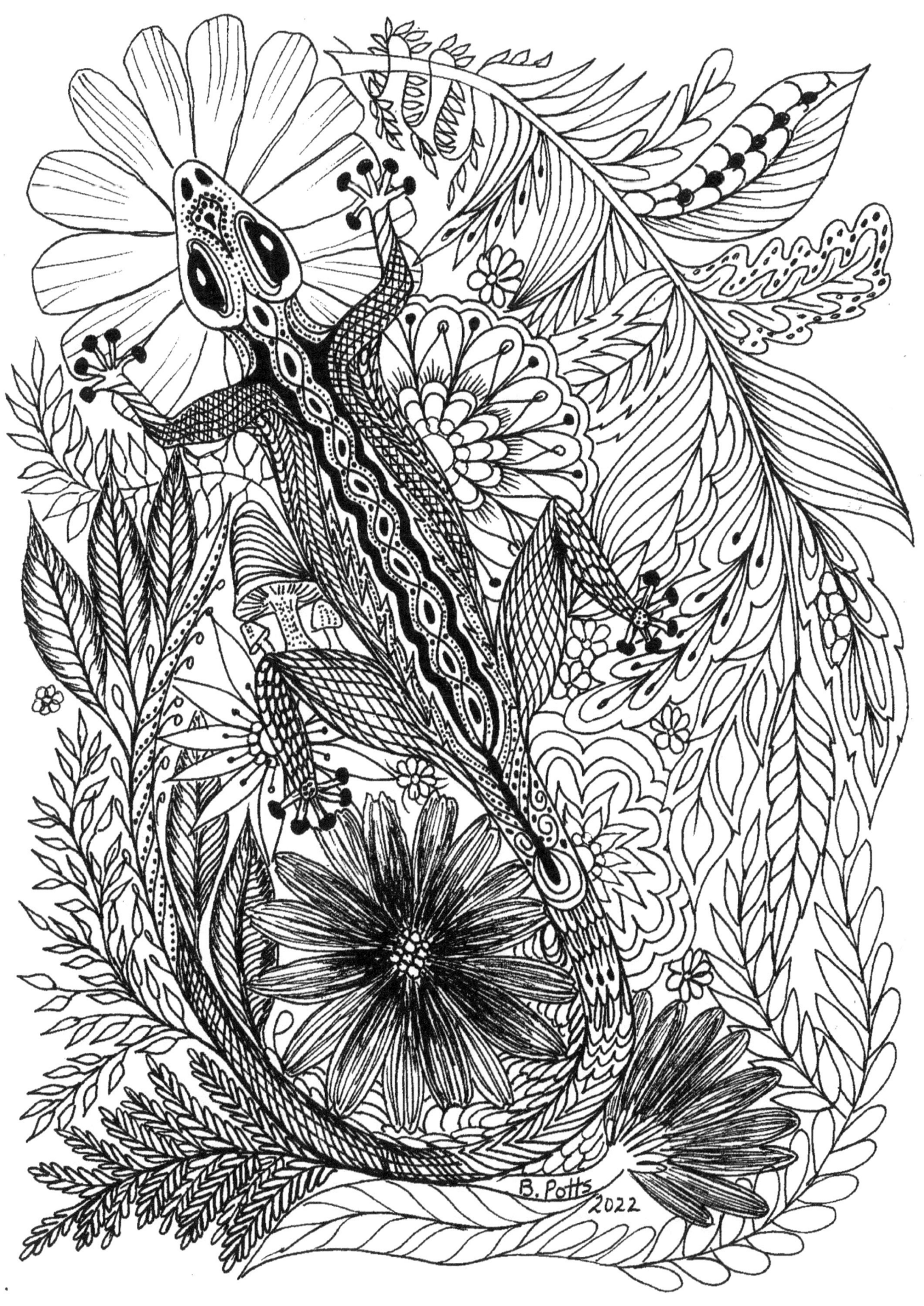

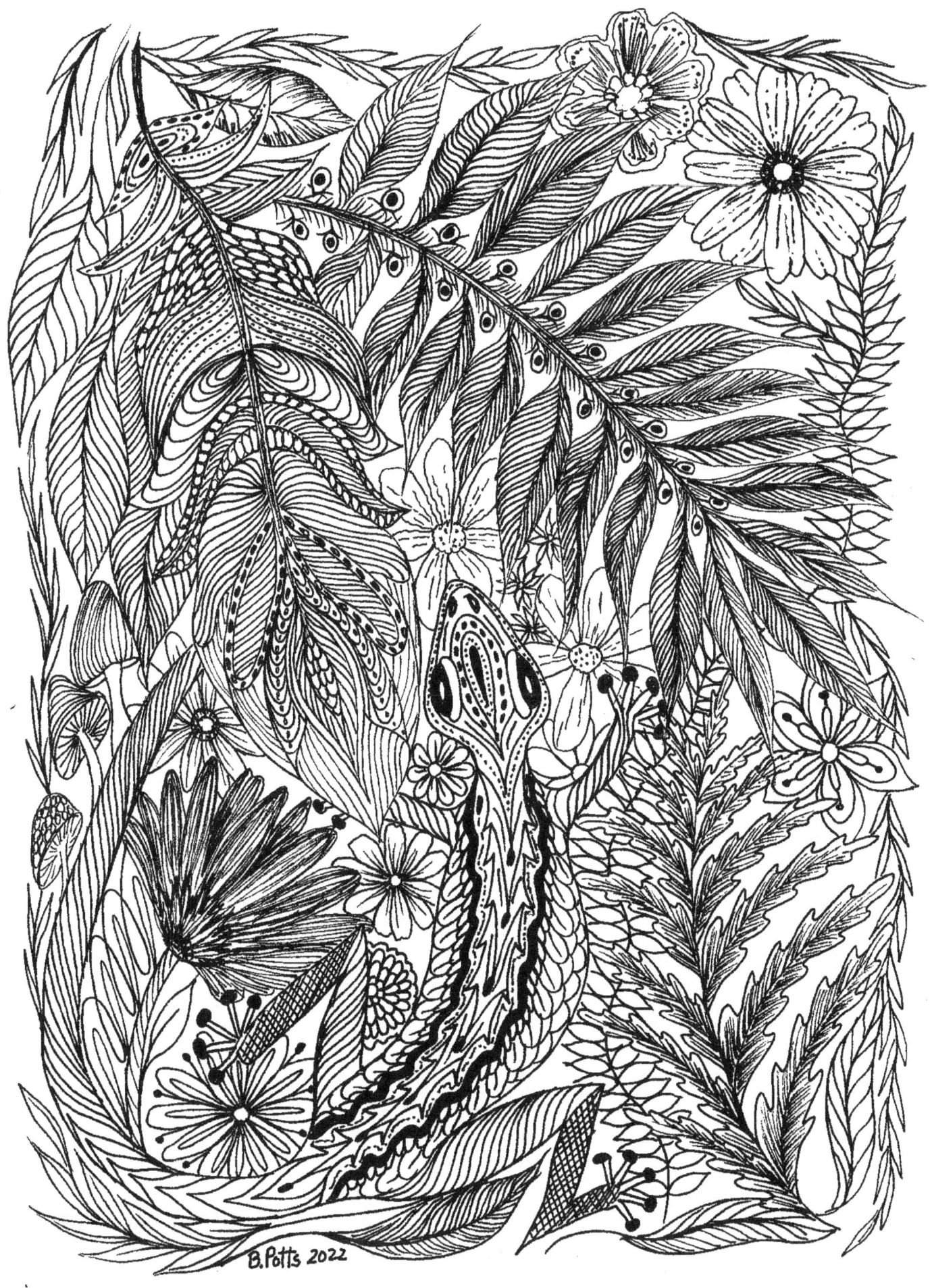

B. Potts 2022

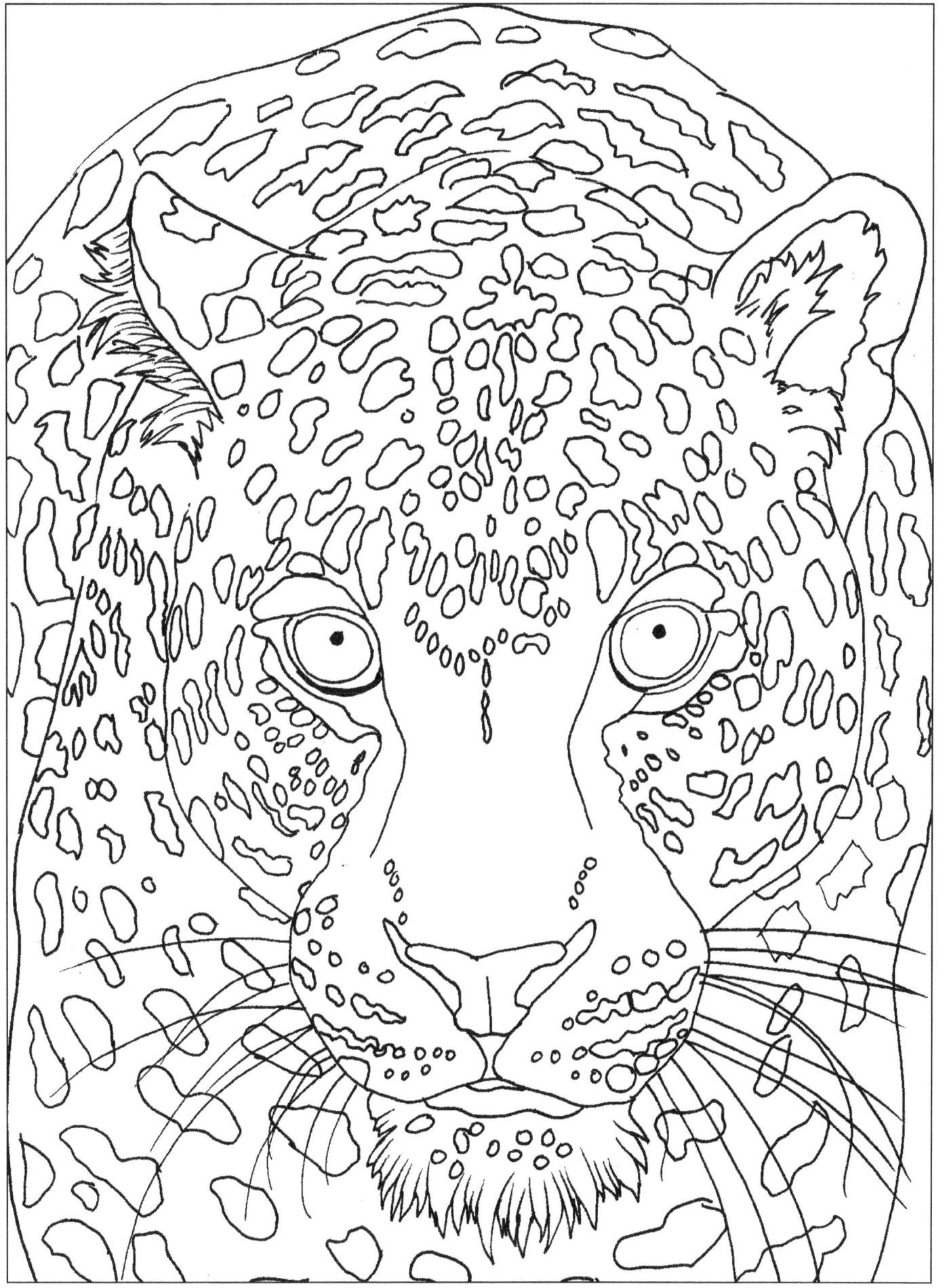

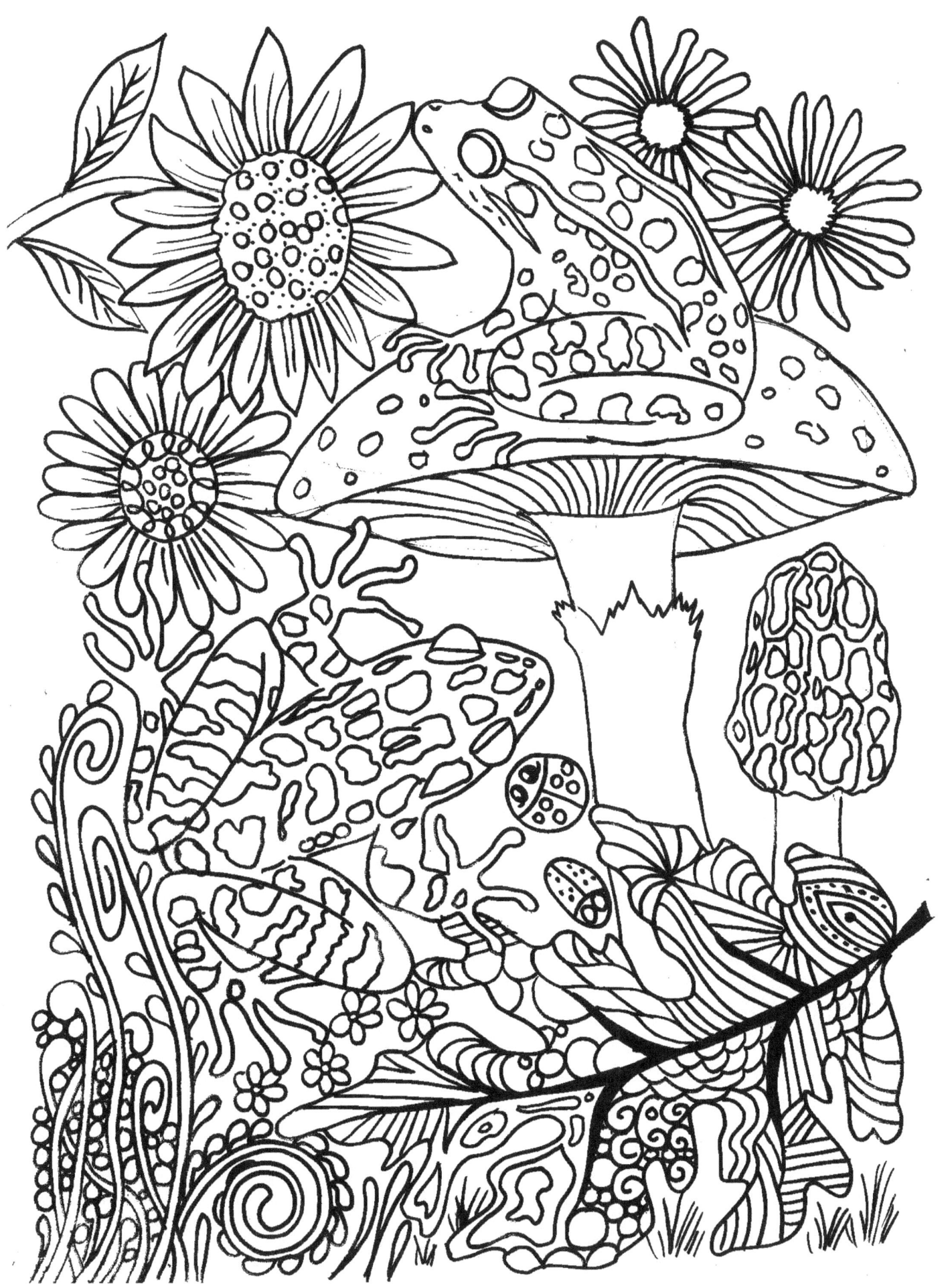

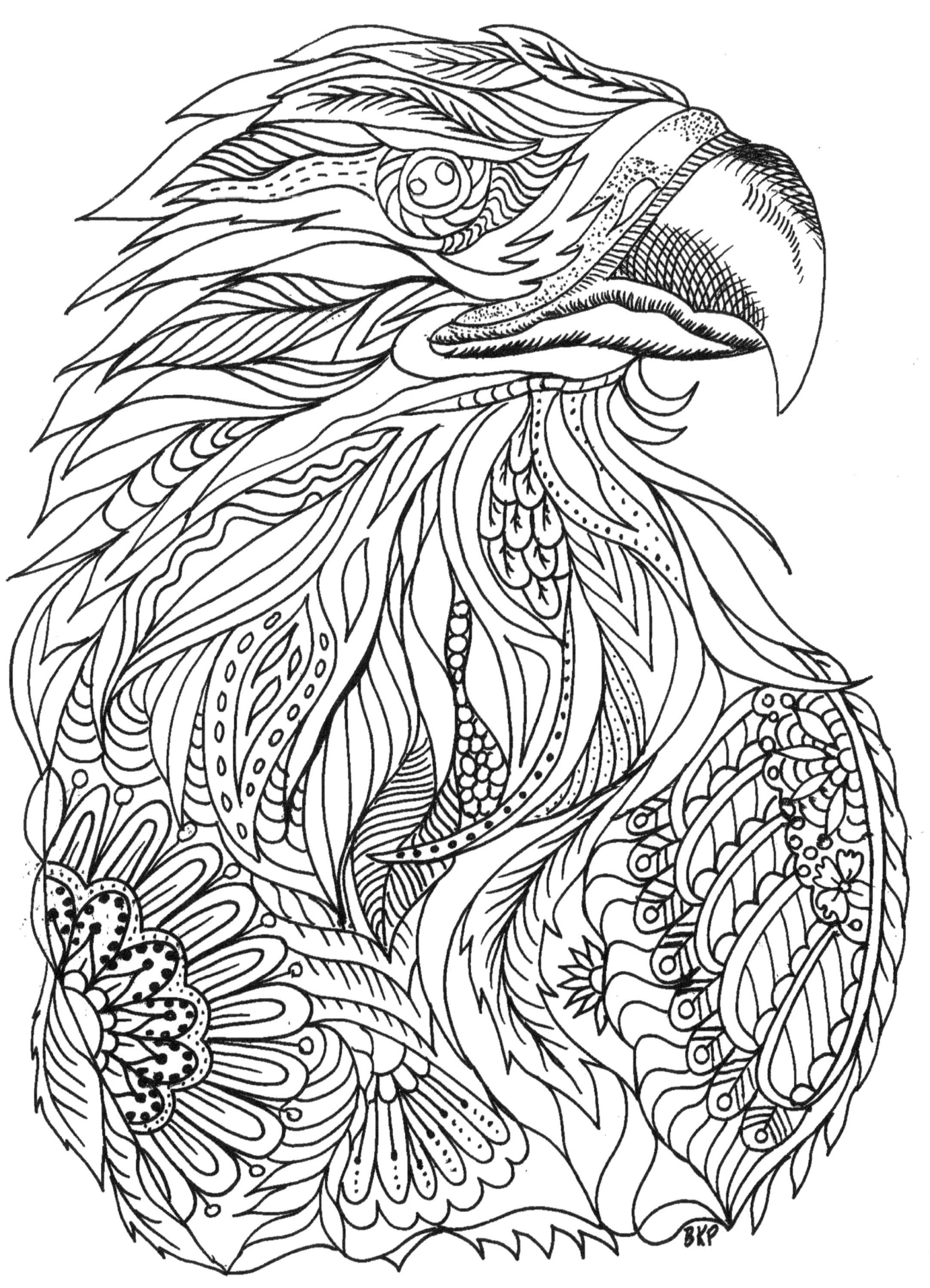

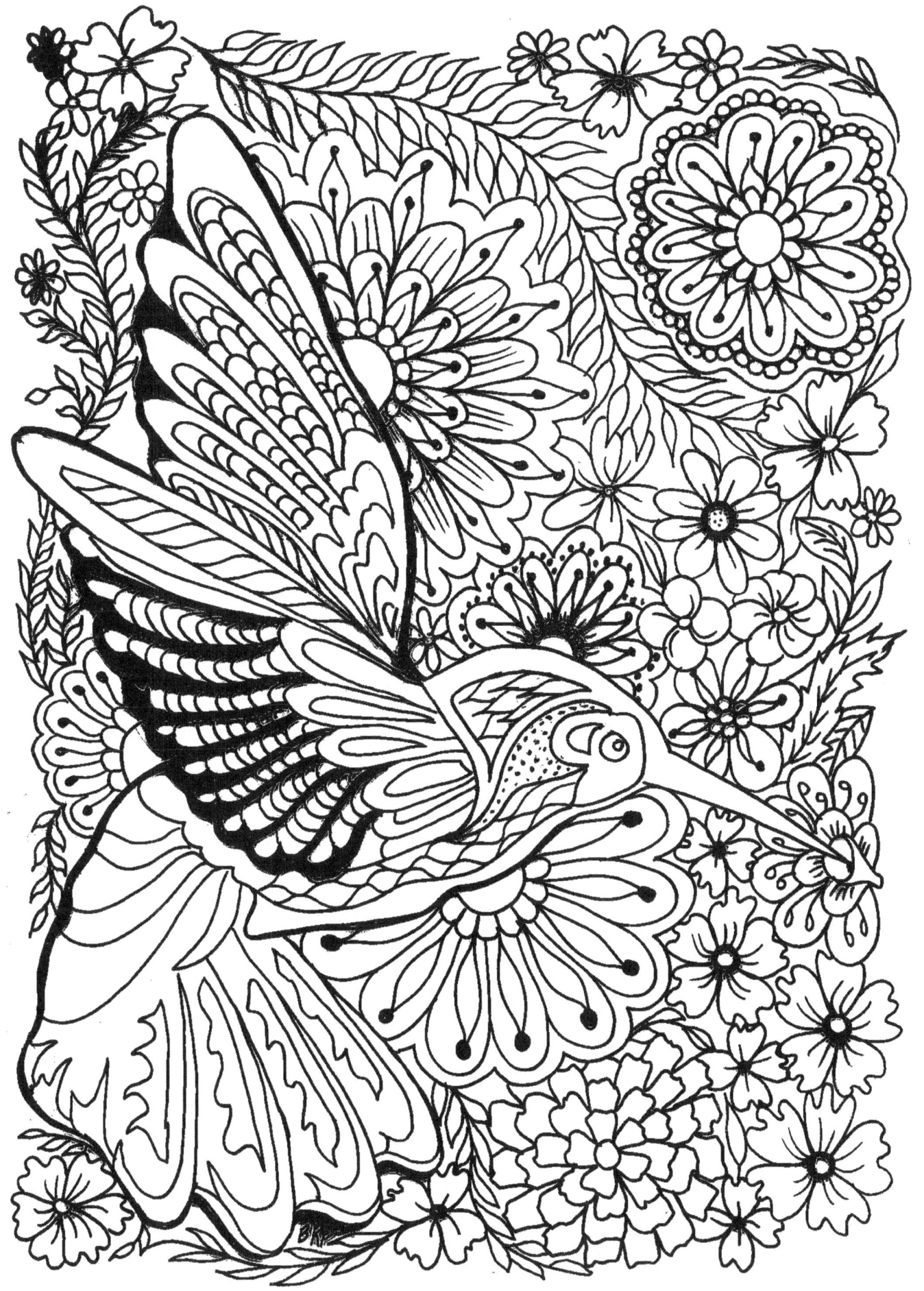

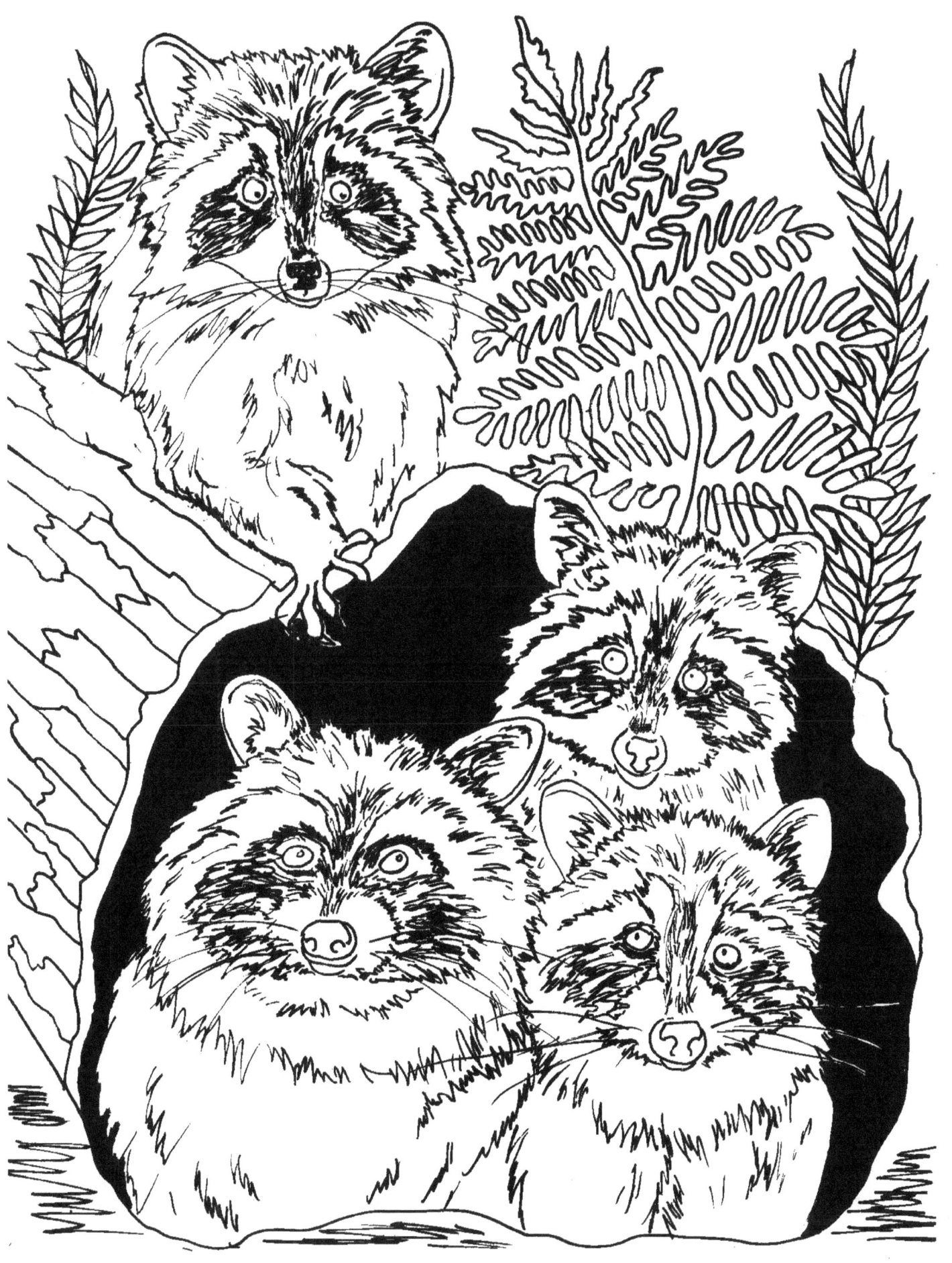

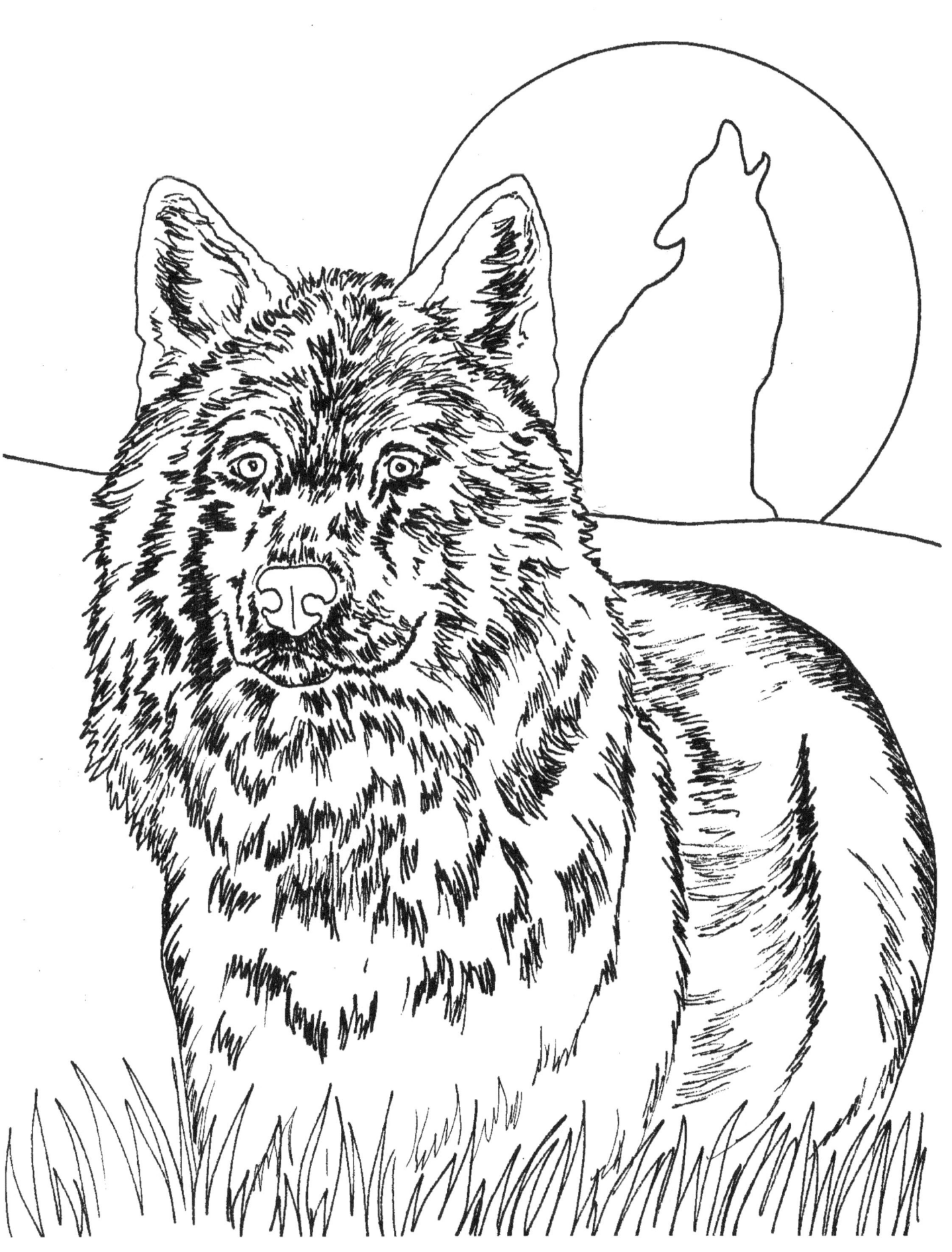

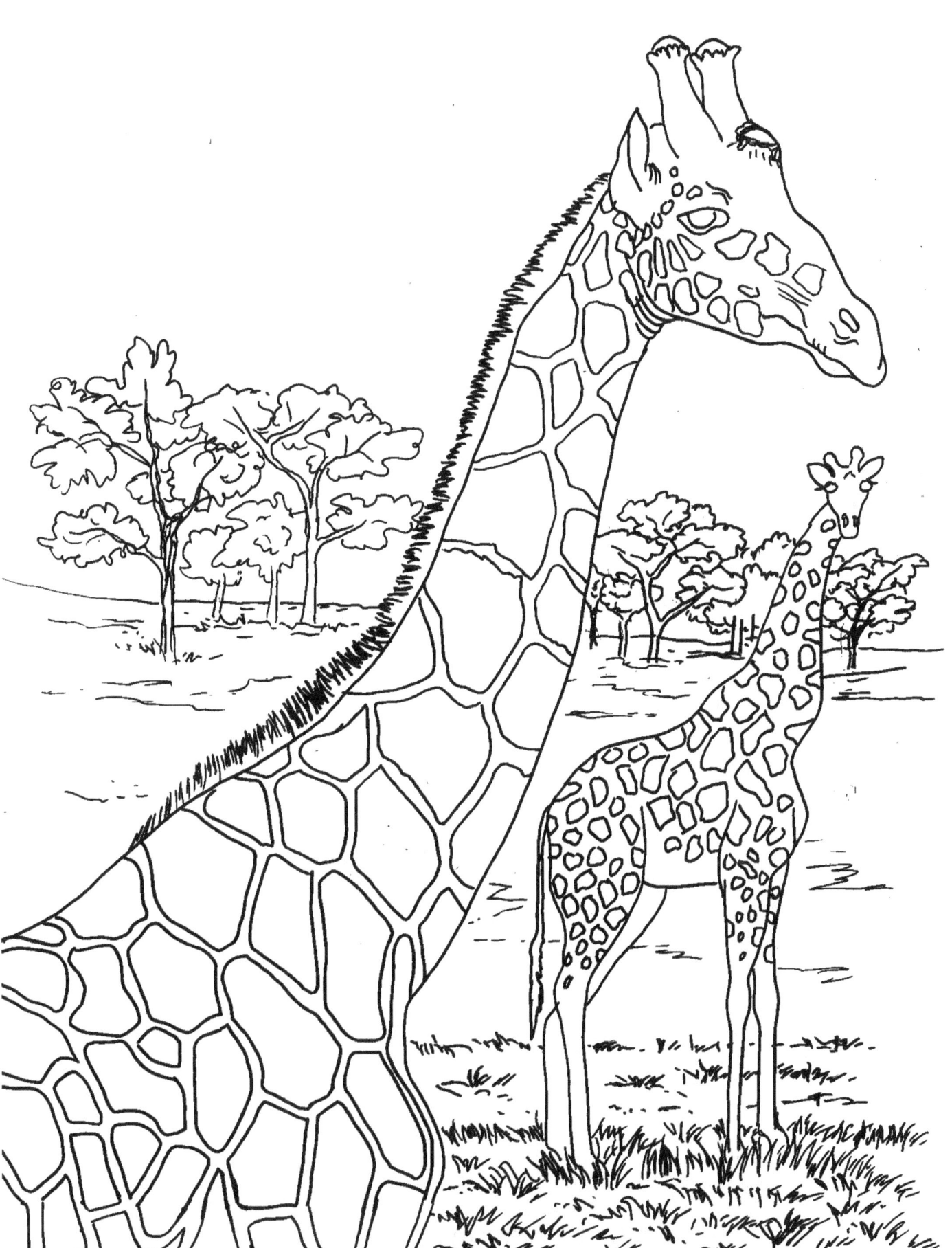

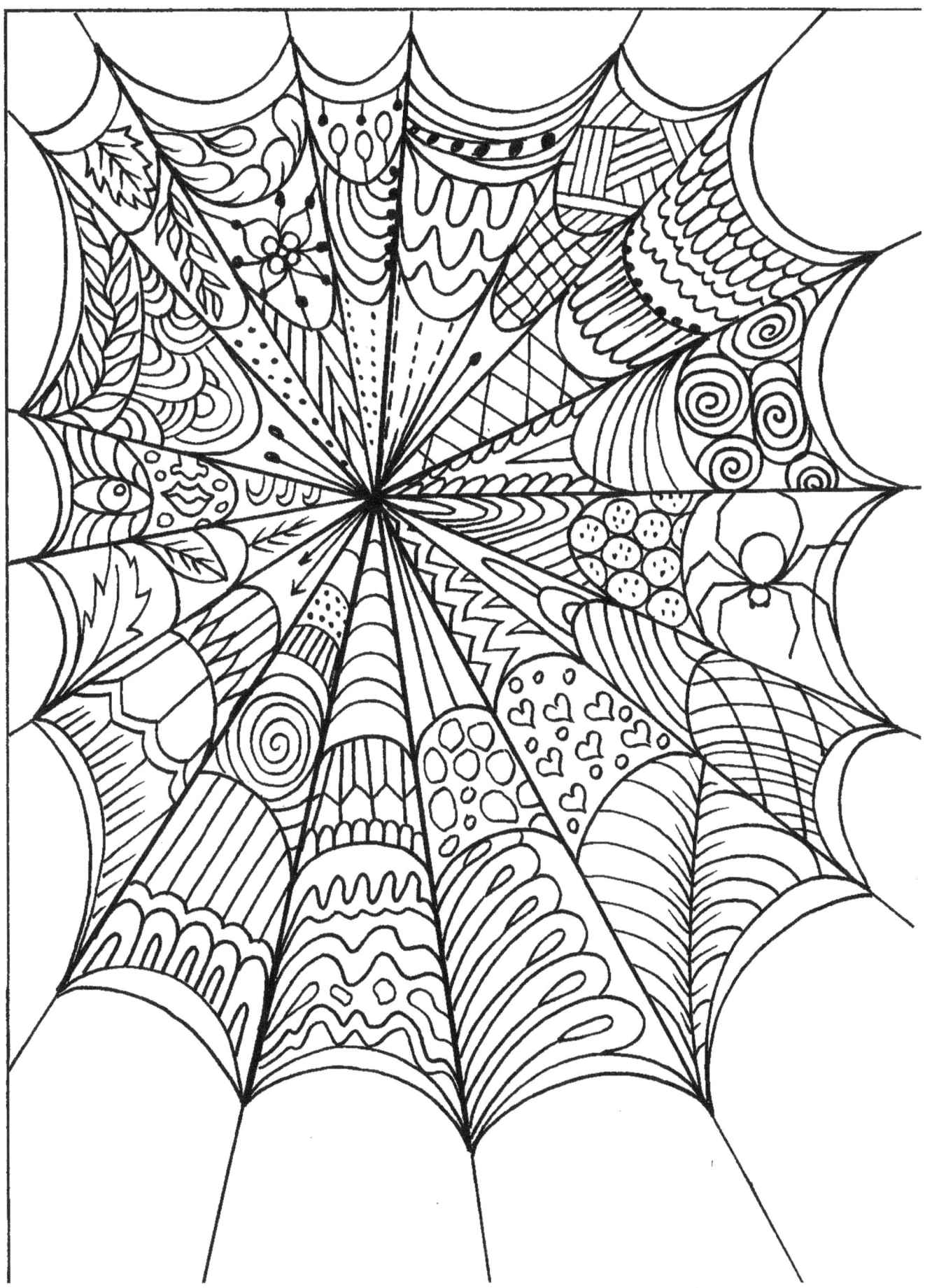

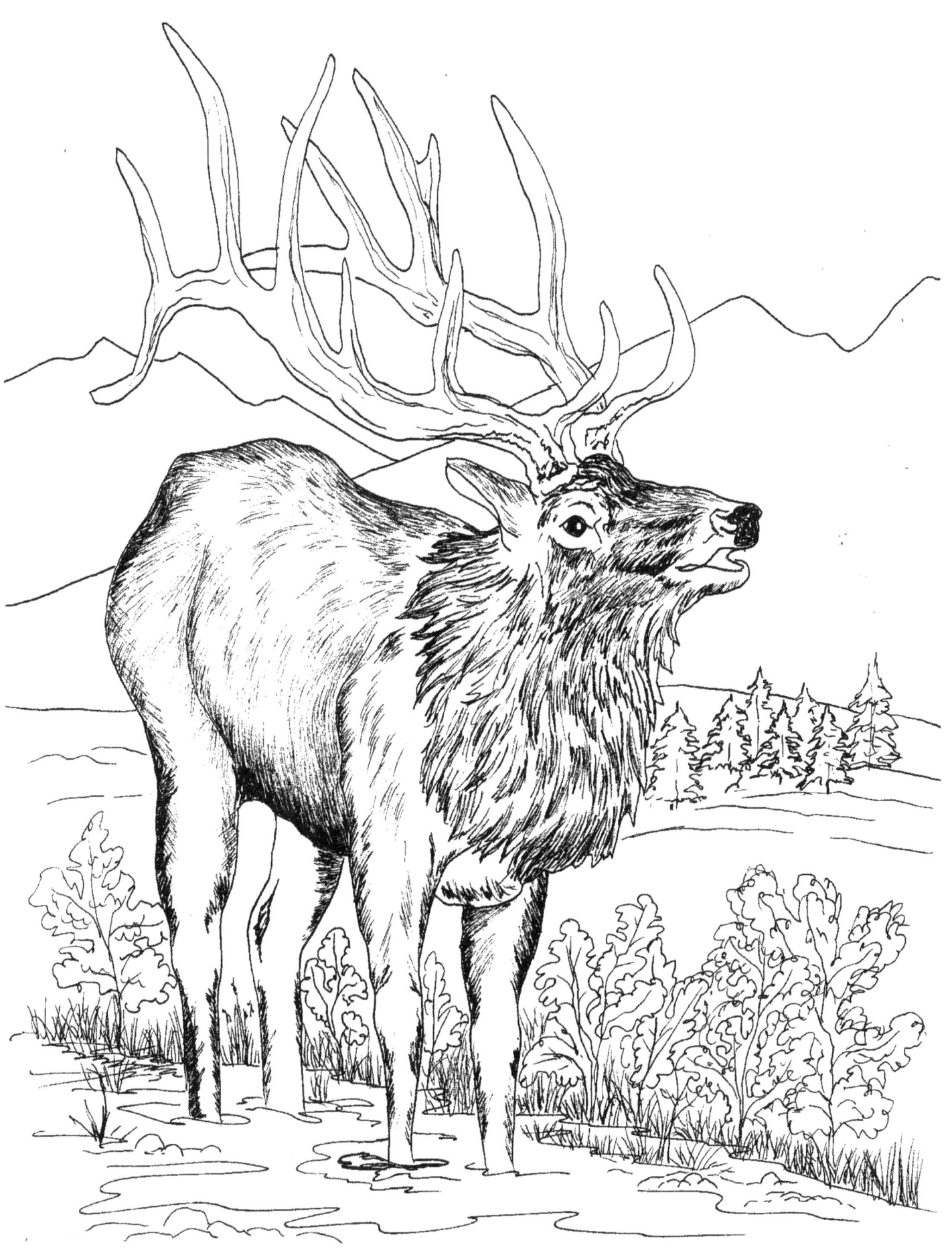

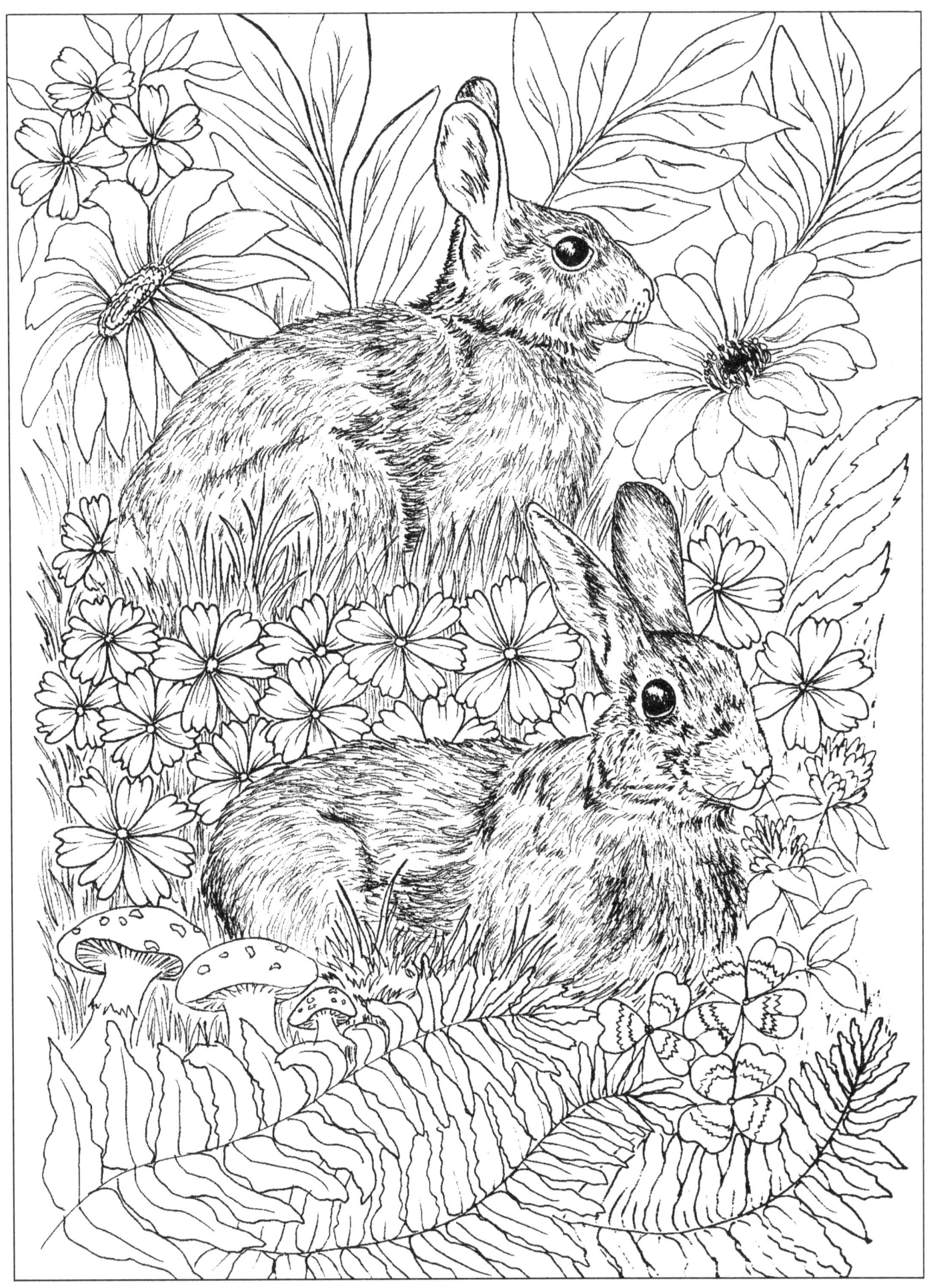

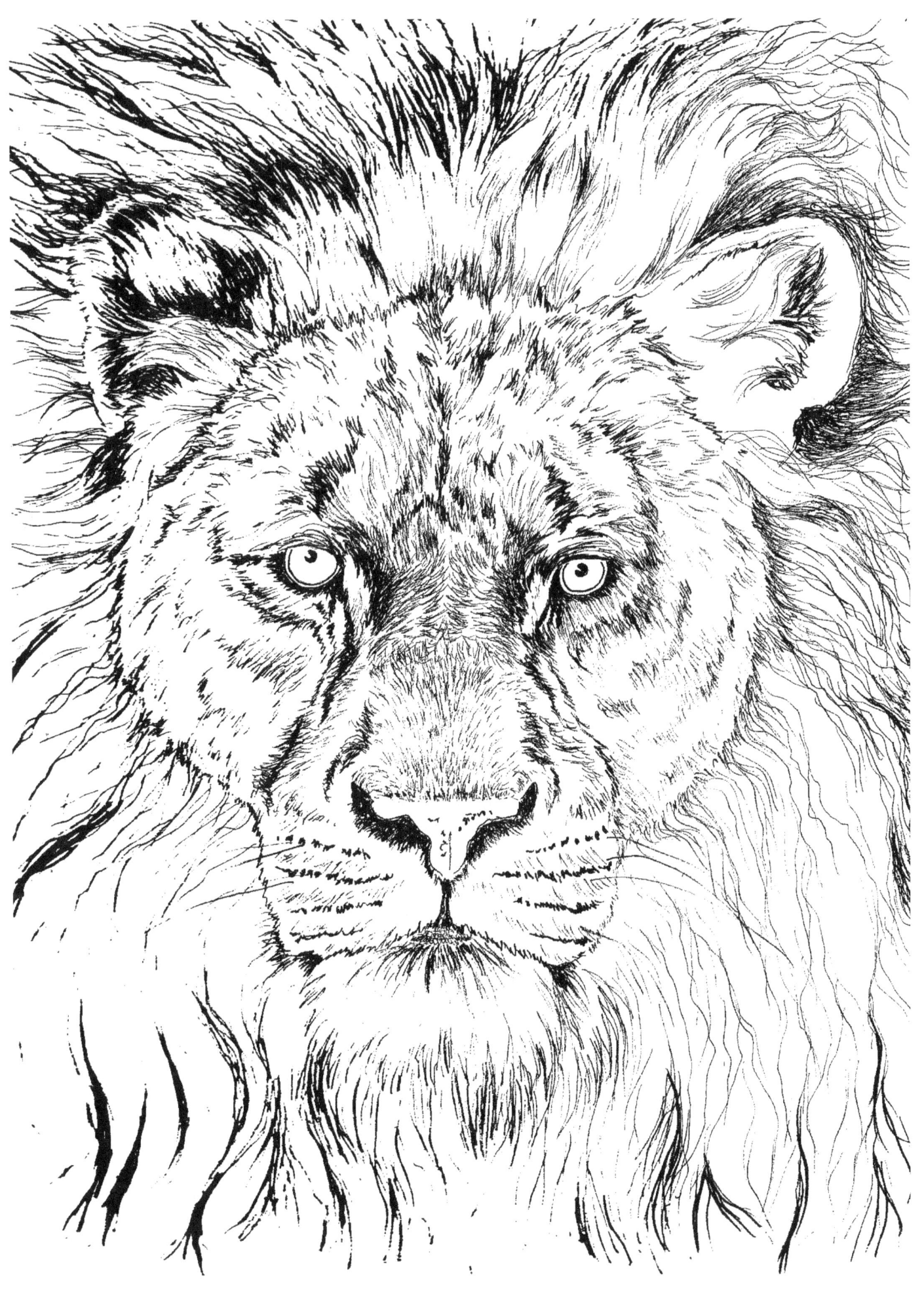

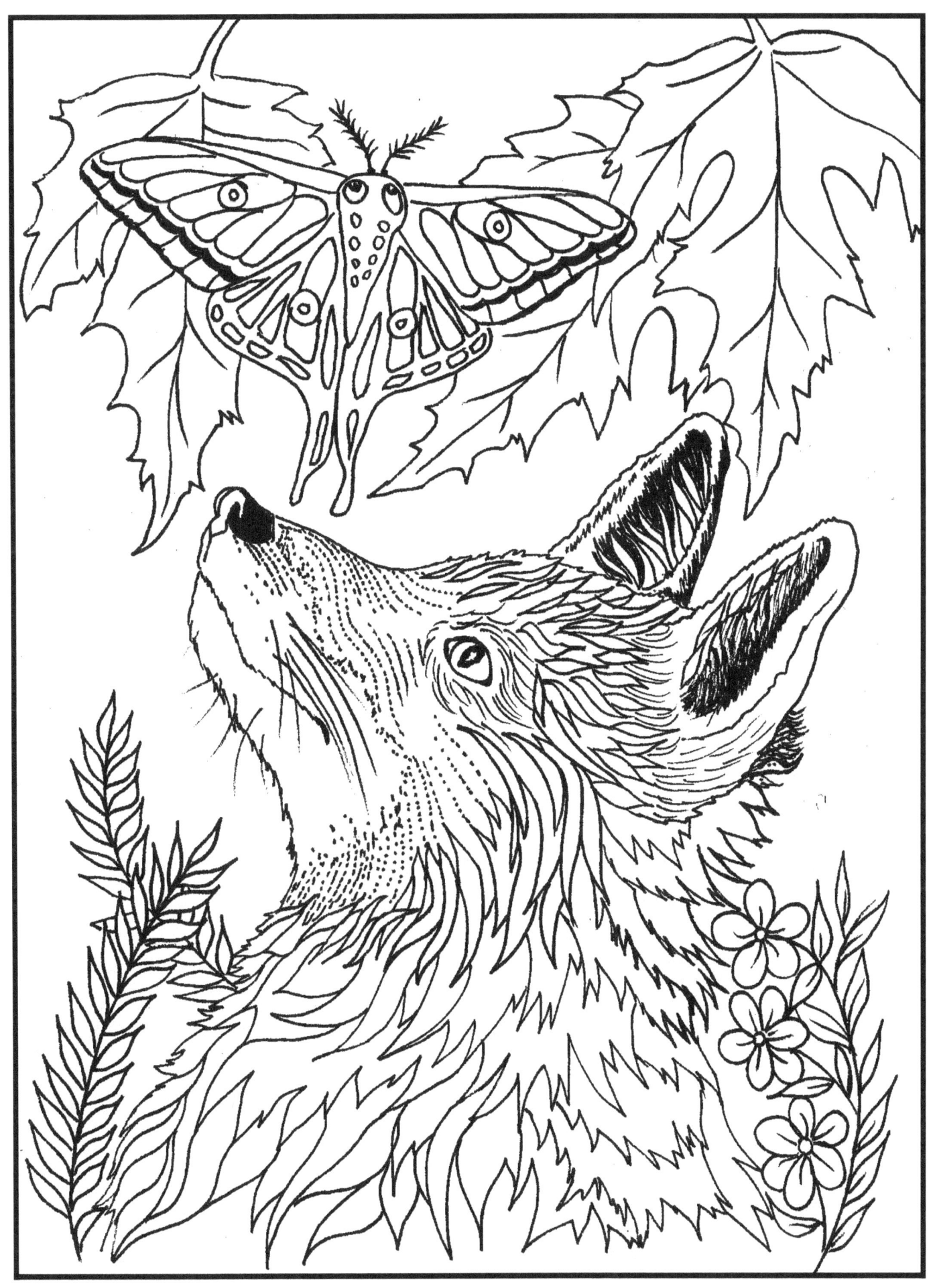

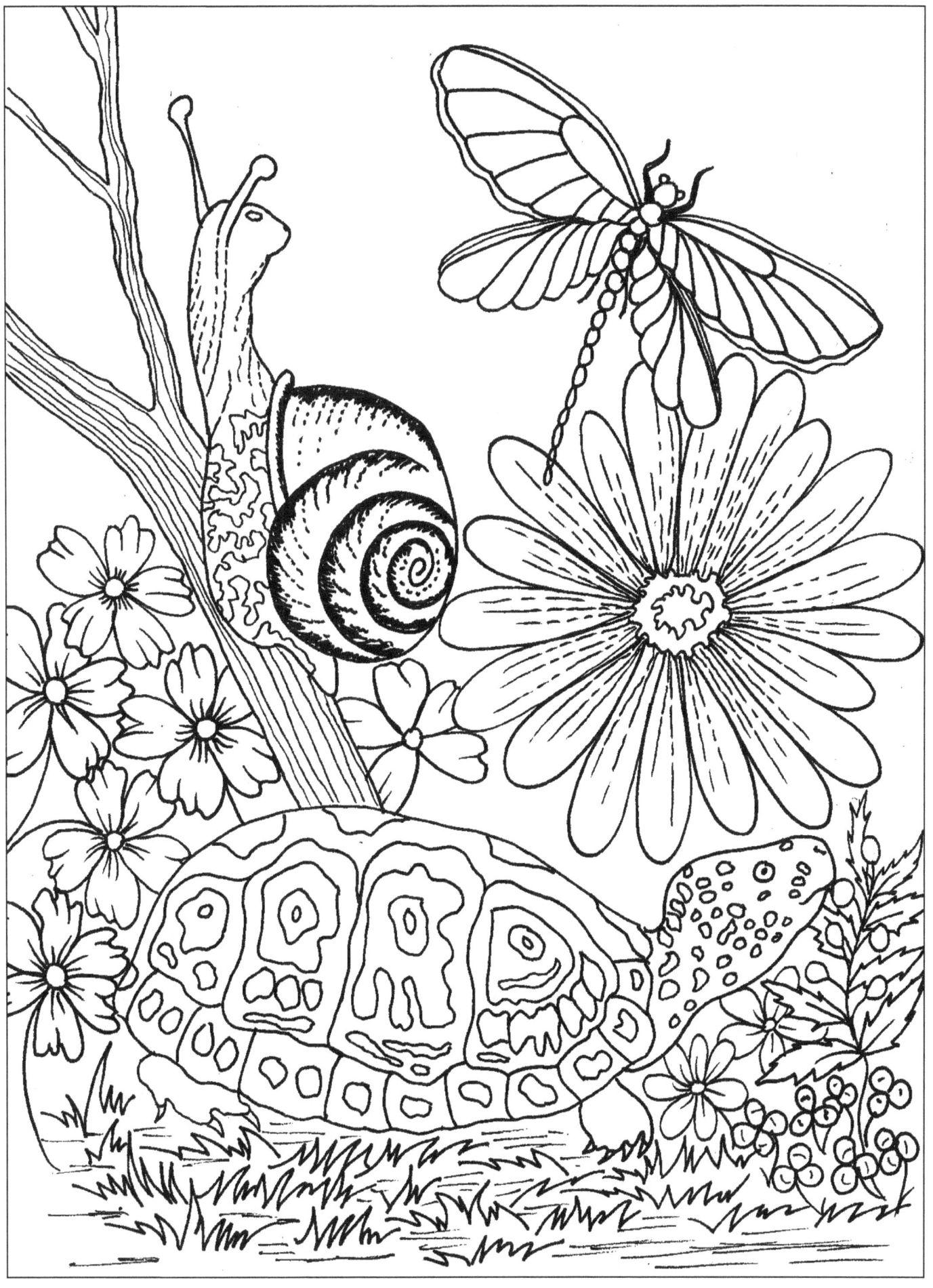

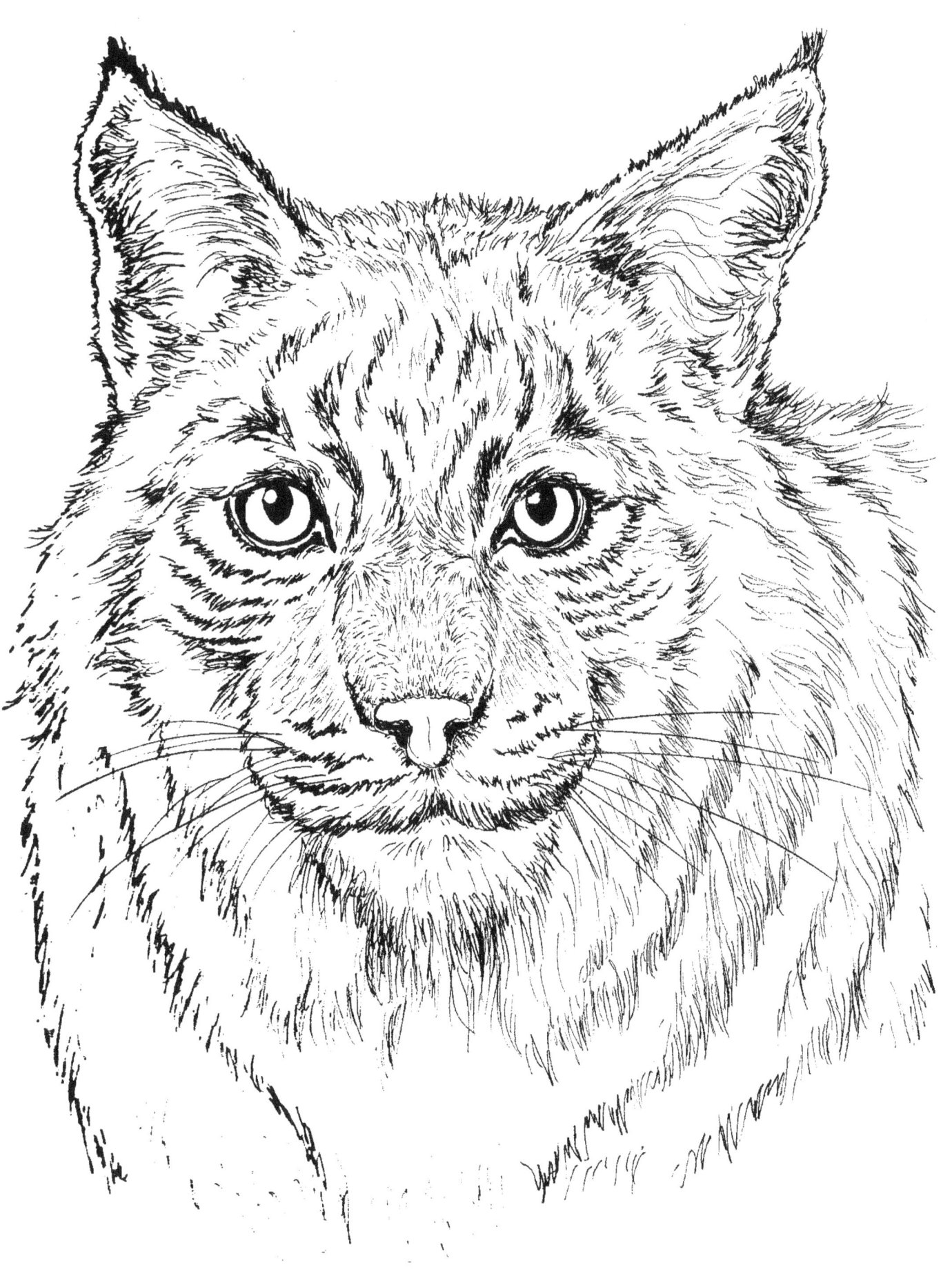

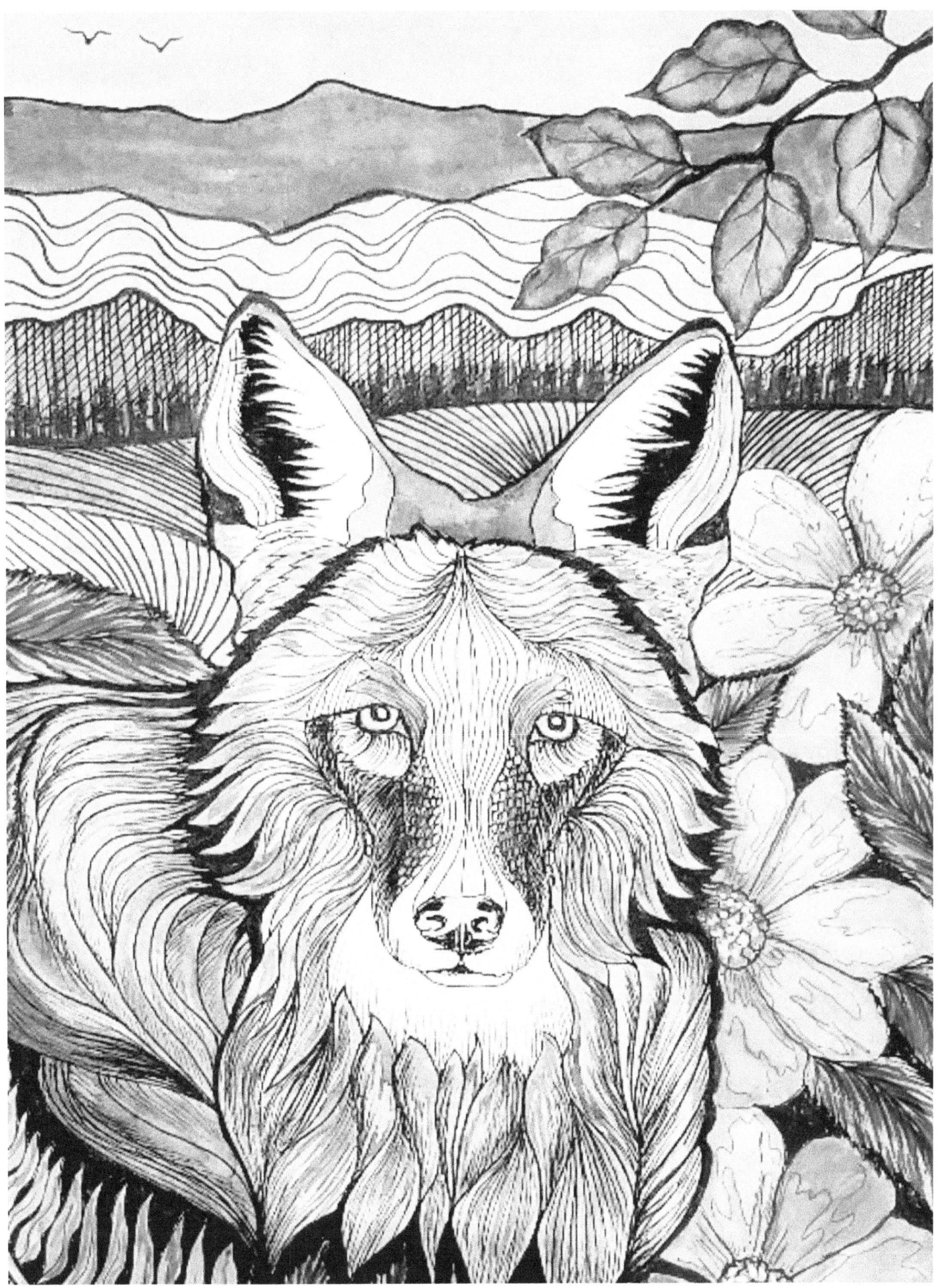

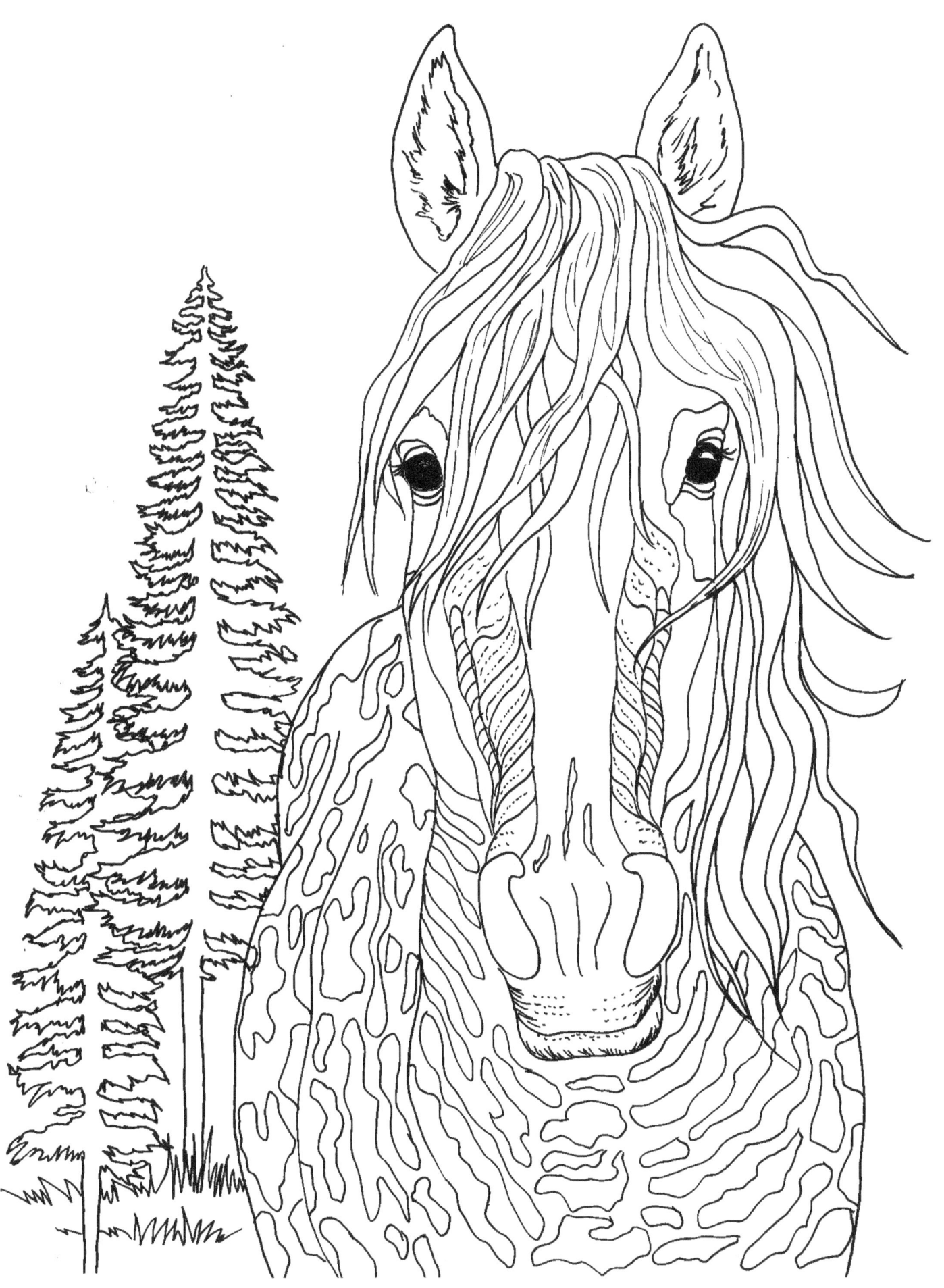

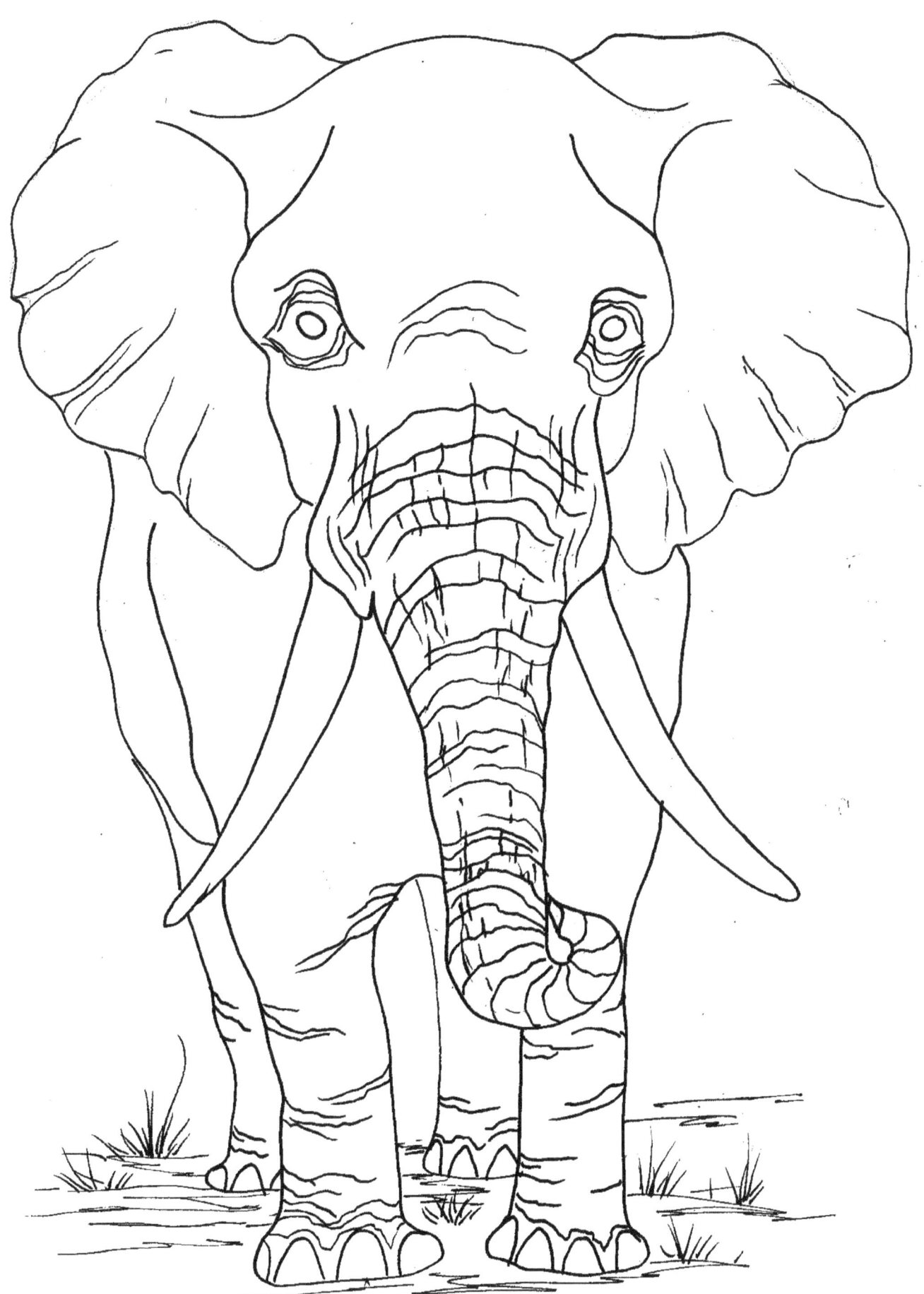

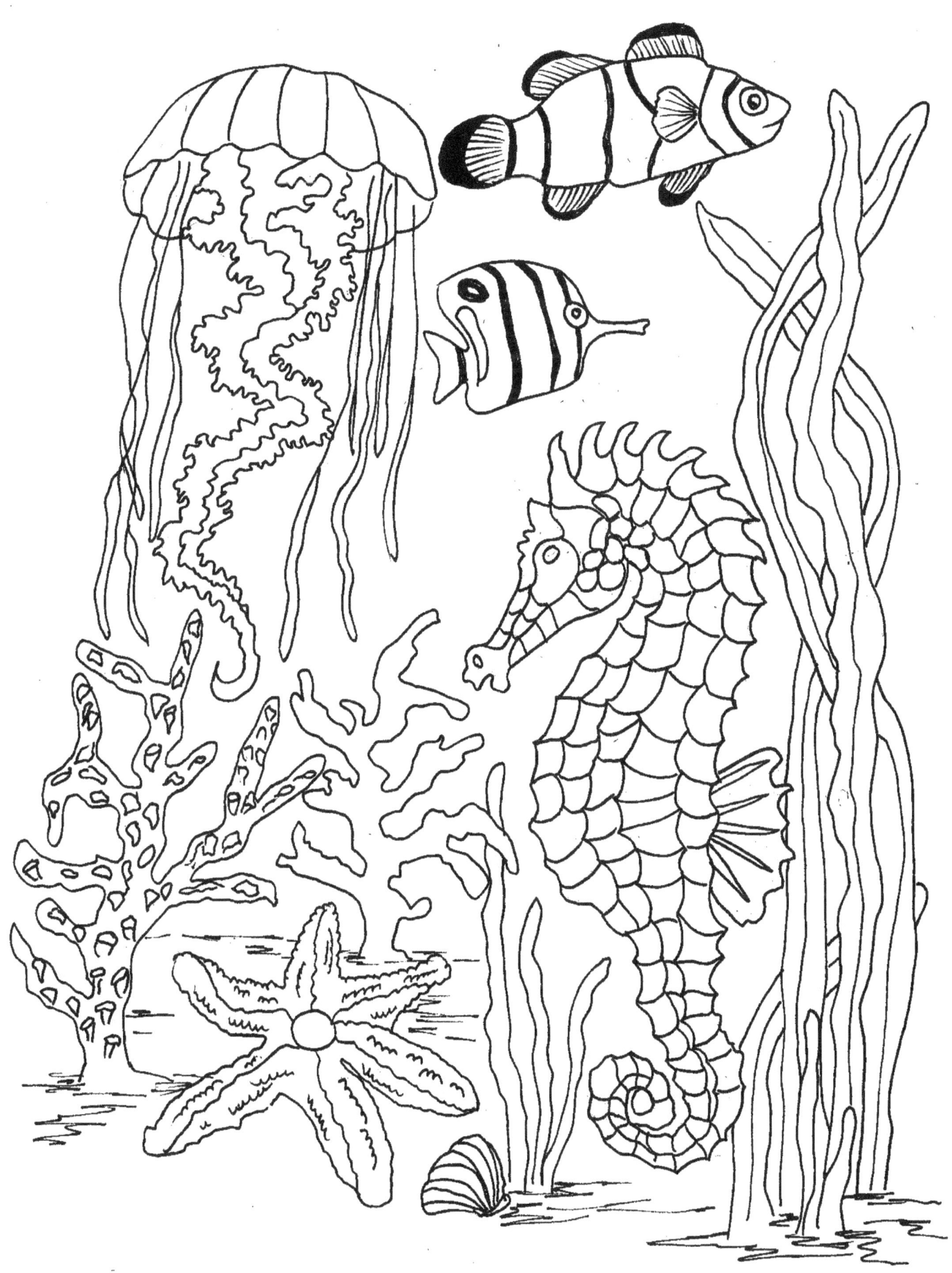

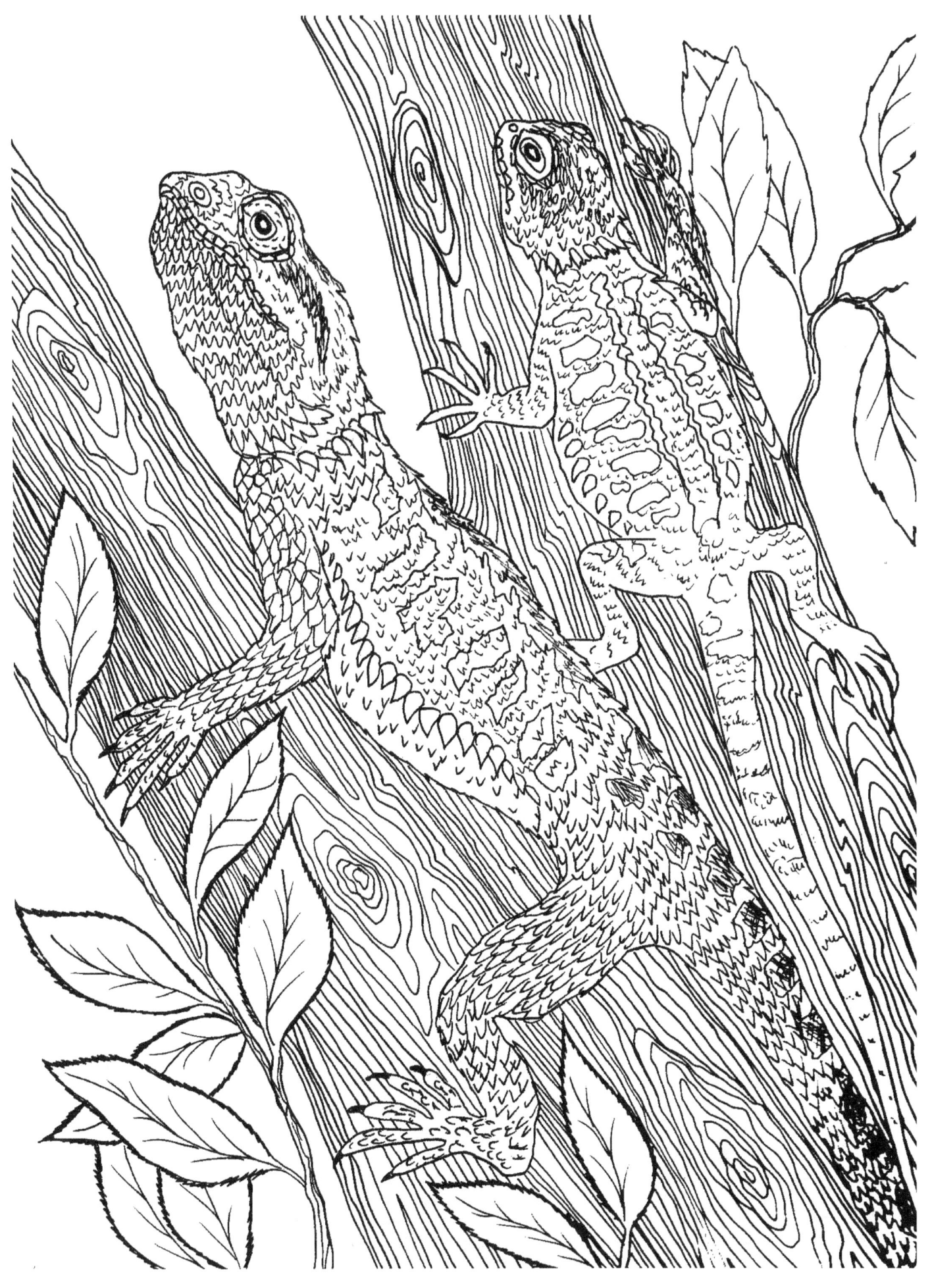

FOR MORE BOOKS TO COLOR VISIT

www.BooksByPotts.com

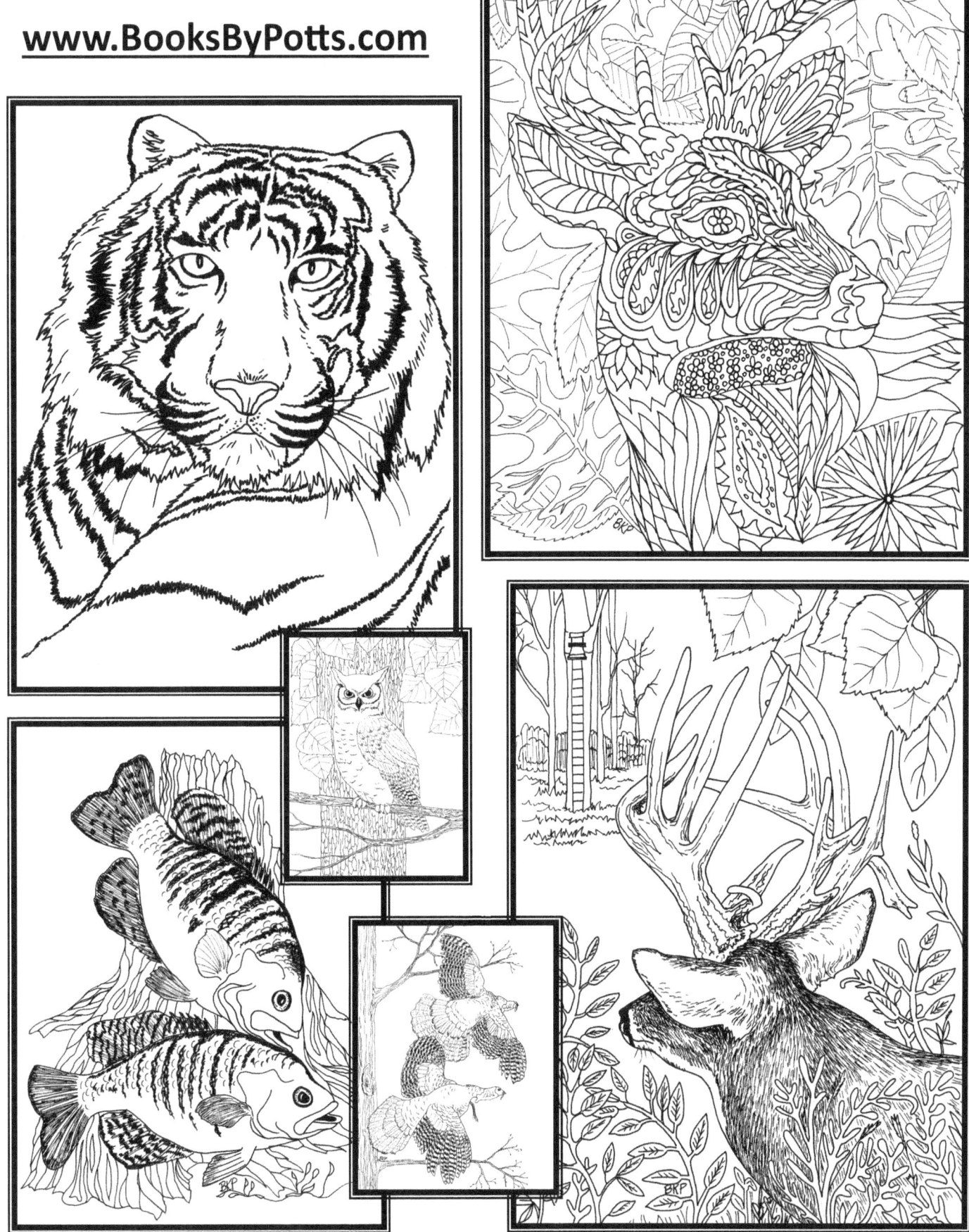